Introductory
BUSINESS LAW

CLEP* Study Guide

All rights reserved. This Study Guide, Book and Flashcards are protected under the US Copyright Law. No part of this book or study guide or flashcards may be reproduced, distributed or stored in a retrieval system, or transmitted in any form or by any means, electronic, mechanical, photocopying, recording, or otherwise, without the prior written permission of the publisher Breely Crush Publishing, LLC.

© 2019 Breely Crush Publishing, LLC

*CLEP is a registered trademark of the College Entrance Examination Board which does not endorse this book.

971073118143

Copyright ©2003 - 2019, Breely Crush Publishing, LLC.

All rights reserved.

This Study Guide, Book and Flashcards are protected under the US Copyright Law. No part of this publication may be reproduced, distributed or stored in a retrieval system, or transmitted in any form or by any means, electronic, mechanical, photocopying, recording, or otherwise, without the prior written permission of the publisher Breely Crush Publishing, LLC.

Published by Breely Crush Publishing, LLC
10808 River Front Parkway
South Jordan, UT 84095
www.breelycrushpublishing.com

ISBN-10: 1-61433-018-2
ISBN-13: 978-1-61433-018-9

Printed and bound in the United States of America.

*CLEP is a registered trademark of the College Entrance Examination Board which does not endorse this book.

Table of Contents

Origins of Law 1
American Legal System and Procedures 5
Constitutional Law 6
Federalism 11
Types of Law 11
Jurisdiction 11
Types of Courts 12
Judges 13
Juries 14
Examination 15
Due Process of Law 16
Assault and Battery 16
Contracts 17
The Six Elements of a Contract 17
Third Party Contracts 21
Obligations 22
Condequentialism 23
Validity of Contracts 24
Voidable Contracts 24
Duress 25
Consideration 25
Mutual Agreement 26
Acceptance 27
Capacity 28
Legality 29
Joint Obligations 29
Termination of an Offer 29
Mistakes of Law 31
Unilateral Mistake 32
Mistake as to the Identity of a Party 32
Mistake as to the Possibility of Performance 33
Mistake as to the Subject Matter 33
Statute of Frauds 33
Breach of Contract 34
Cancellation and Restitution 36
Scope and Meaning of Contracts 37
Assignment and Delegation 37
Illegal Contracts 39
Discharge of Contracts 40

Agency	*41*
Employment Contracts and Law	*42*
Title VII	*43*
Affirmative Action	*43*
Comparable Worth	*44*
ADA	*45*
OSHA	*45*
FLSA	*45*
Sales Contracts	*46*
Torts	*47*
Property Law	*49*
Personal Property	*50*
Product Liability	*51*
Employee Liability	*53*
Insider Trading	*53*
Whistle Blowing	*54*
Commercial Paper	*56*
Consumer Protection	*56*
UCC	*58*
EPA	*59*
CERCLA	*59*
Endangered Species Act	*60*
Clean Air Act	*60*
Clean Water Act	*61*
Terms to Know	*61*
Sample Test Questions	*63*
Test-Taking Strategies	*115*
What Your Score Means	*116*
Test Preparation	*116*
Legal Note	*117*

Origins of Law

In early times, the first known legal codes were written by the Babylonians and Hebrews who developed their own brand of law when the concept of law was first recognized. These first legal codes were then taken up and further developed by the Romans. Credited with actually developing one of the first **legal codes** in about 2000 B.C. was King Dungi of Sumer (the area today is known as Iraq). We know of these first legal codes because they were later adopted by Hammurabi (1792-1750 B.C.), the sixth king of Babylon, and incorporated into his famous set of written laws that today is known as the Code Of Hammurabi. Written and preserved on rock columns, this code established crimes and their corrections. Punishment was based on physical retaliation or lex talionis ("an eye for an eye"). The severity of punishment depended on class standing: if you were a free man you would only lose a limb; if you were a slave, you lost your life.

The next set of ancient legal codes that survived is the Mosaic Code of the Israelites (1200 B.C.). This is when God entered into an agreement or contract with the tribes of Israel when they decided to obey His Law. The 613 laws of the Old Testament, including the Ten Commandments, presented by Moses, were obeyed in order to receive God's special care and protection. The Mosaic Code is not only the foundation of Judeo-Christian moral teachings, but it is the basis for our U.S. legal system today (In God We Trust). The laws against murder, theft, perjury and adultery have carried through thousands of years and founded our U.S. legal system.

During the Dark Ages, which lasted about 500 years after the fall of Rome (500-1000 A.D.), all early formal legal codes were lost. During this period, dark magic, superstition and fear of the satanic black arts dominated all ways of thinking. Not until the Norman conquest of England in 1066, did **common law** grow and helped standardize law and justice throughout the land. Before the Norman Conquest, what legal system there was among the English (Anglo-Saxons) and throughout Europe was decentralized. This means that each county known as the **Shire** was divided into units called hundreds, which were groups of 100 families. Each hundred was divided further into 10 families called **tithings**. The head of law enforcement of the Shire was called a Reeve. (The shire reeve is embodied today in the county sheriff.) Usually within smaller groups throughout the land the tithings maintained and dealt with most of the minor disputes that cropped up among the families.

The present English system of law came into existence during the reign of Henry II (1154-1189). Henry was the first to use traveling judges, better known today as circuit judges. These judges followed specific routes known as circuits and heard cases that previously had been under the jurisdiction of local courts. Juries also began to develop about this time and they consisted of groups of landholders whom judges called on to decide on the facts of cases; later they were also relied upon to investigate the crimes the accused were supposed to have committed.

Times were hard back in the days of medieval England and criminal charges were often decided by what was then called an **ordeal**. A trial by fire had the accused hold out their hand where a hot iron was placed. If the burn did not heal properly, the accused was considered guilty. In a trial by combat, the defendant could challenge his accuser to a dual; however, the accuser could obtain an alternate to fight his battles.

Eventually, royal prosecutors were established as key players in the court proceedings. These representatives of the Crown submitted evidence and brought witnesses to testify before the jury. Few formal procedures existed at this time, but the prosecutors and judges could intimidate the witnesses as well as the jurors whenever they felt it was necessary to do so. The progress of these judicial processes was the beginning of what we know today as common law.

Just as it is used today, common law refers to the law of the land and England held on to the Anglo-Saxton concepts. For example, common law defined murder as the unlawful killing of another human being with planned malice. For someone to be found guilty of murder there had to be two things involved and they are: (1) the planning of a crime and (2) the intent to kill the victim with spite or hatred. Over time though, this general definition proved inadequate, because each situation was different, even though the intent may have still been the same. Judges began to differentiate the causes of death and needed to bring the law closer to the realities of human behavior. Deaths were determined to be caused by passion (manslaughter), negligence (involuntary manslaughter), rage (second degree murder), or cunning (capital or first-degree murder). If a person killed a person while committing another crime, such as robbery, he or she would be convicted of a capital murder even if that murder was unintentional. Common law continued to evolve because each case of murder was different and warranted different degrees of punishment.

Before the American Revolution, the colonies were still under British rule and the laws were handed down by the British judges. Once the colonies acquired their independence they started changing the laws to better fit what was going on in their own colonies. State legislatures standardized common-law crimes like murder, burglary, rape and arson by putting them into statutory form in criminal codes. Common law principles started to change due to these conversions and examples of these changes can be found in the Massachusetts statute defining arson. The common-law definition of arson is "the malicious burning of another" and Massachusetts took the definition a step further by adding "the willful and malicious setting fire to, or burning of any building or contents thereof even if they were burned by the owner." Through the years, whenever common law proved to be inadequate to deal with certain legal situations and moral issues, laws were changed to better handle each situation.

There are many different ways to classify laws and we need these classifications to help us understand the law better. Law can be divided into two very broad categories, **criminal law** and **civil law**. One way to narrow the field is to remember that anything that is not criminal law is civil law. **Civil law** includes legal areas like property law, which governs transfer and ownership of property, and contract law, which is the law of personal agreements. **Tort law** is the law of personal wrongs and damages, and is similar in form and intent to criminal law. A **tort** is a civil action in which an individual asks to be compensated for personal harm done to him or her. **Harm** can be either physical or mental harm and can include acts like assault, trespassing, battery, and invasion of privacy. Other forms of harm can be **libel**, false and injurious writings, and **slander**, false and injurious statements. These torts can occur when someone is injured by the actions of another, even if they have not been found guilty of a criminal act. The standard of evidence for a finding is less in civil cases than it is in criminal cases. To be found guilty in a criminal act, the proof must be beyond a reasonable doubt, while in civil cases, preponderance of the evidence is all the proof needed. A civil law violation can also happen when someone else's behavior indirectly causes injury or death. Since many torts are similar to criminal acts, a person can be held responsible for both civil and criminal liability. There are also differences between criminal and civil law. Criminal law gives the state the power to protect the public from harm by punishing those who threaten the social order of things. The most important thing to remember about civil and criminal law is their purposes are basically the same and this is to control people's behavior by setting down limits to what a person can and cannot do, both of these accomplished through state-imposed sanctions. In tort law, the harm is considered a private wrong with the main concern being that the victim is compensated for the harm done to him or her, usually by monetary compensation. When a criminal act has occurred, the state initiates the legal proceedings by bringing charges and prosecuting the violator. When it's determined that a criminal law has been broken, the state imposes punishment, which usually consists of the imprisonment of the violator.

Criminal law can be further broken down into two forms of crimes, misdemeanors and felonies. Felonies are more serious crimes such as murder, rape and burglary. Crimes such as unarmed assaults, battery, petty larceny and disturbing the peace are all considered misdemeanors. In most states, felonies are crimes punishable by death or imprisonment of more than one year. Misdemeanors are punishable with up to a year in prison, probation, or a fine to compensate for damages.

Crimes are also classified as **mala in se** and **mala prohibitum**. Mala in se are crimes about as old as time itself, or for as long as man has existed, and are referred to as natural law. Wrongs like rape, murder and assault, the taking of and harming another person's property, malicious damage and trespassing are all considered mala in se. Mala prohibitum are statutory crimes and violate laws that reflect social values and public opinion. Offenses like drug use, public drunkenness and prostitution are considered to upset the standards of morality. Mala prohibitum are more difficult to define because so many people are willing to engage in many of these behaviors.

Substantive criminal law is the written code that defines crimes and their punishments. In the U.S. state and federal governments have developed their own unique criminal codes. Even if the codes differ from state to state, the underlying definitions are still basically the same, to enforce social control.

The main purpose of criminal law is to control the behavior of people within its jurisdiction. Criminal law is a statement of written rules that people must conform to and defines which behaviors are allowable and which are not. Criminal law also sets forth punishments to be administered to persons found guilty of committing illegal acts. Every society, no matter where they are, maintains unwritten rules of conduct, universally followed behaviors that are referred to as **norms** and **morals**. Criminal law's function is to control social behavior through its ability to punish and correct law violators. The threat of punishment when breaking the law is designed to prevent people from breaking the law in the first place. During the Middle Ages, public executions made it clear what would happen to people who broke the law. Today, the threat of imprisonment and executions are relayed through the news and other public sources of information.

Our legal system is designed to support and maintain the boundaries of our social system. The law in the U.S. serves out punishments to those who damage or steal property because it needs to protect the activities that sustain our economy. It would be impossible to conduct business through the use of contracts, promissory notes, credit, banking and so on unless the law protected private capital. Maintaining a legal climate in which capitalism can thrive is an underlying goal of U.S. criminal law. Criminal law did not always protect those who had been robbed or had something stolen from them. In early England, if one person cheated another, it was considered a private matter. The Carrier's Case in 1473 changed all that when the court ruled that it was wrong for people to hold and transport property owned by another and keeping the goods for their own purpose was considered theft. Once England recognized that its mercantile trade system could not be sustained if property rights were not protected, the laws had to be changed. To this day, criminal law prohibits such business-related crimes as larceny, fraud, embezzlement and commercial theft. Without the law to protect the free enterprise system, we would not have one.

 American Legal System and Procedures

The fundamental idea of the American legal system is that the law is created by and for the people and made to protect the people, and to secure freedoms. The legal system was developed with the Constitution of the United States as the highest law of the land. The main intention of government is the security of rights and freedoms of the people, such as: freedom of speech; freedom of religion; right to equal protection of the law; and right to due process of law and a fair trial. The U.S. Constitution is known as *the* law of the land and no other source of law can conflict with it. Any statute or federal, state, or judicial decision, cannot be enforced if the statute contradicts or conflicts with the Constitution. The U.S. Supreme Court is responsible for the final interpretation of the meaning of the Constitution.

Four sources of law combine to create the laws of America.

- The most important source of American law comes from **The Constitution** of the United States and **constitutional law**. Constitutional Law is based on a formal document (federal or state constitutions) that describes wide-ranging powers.
- The second source of American law is the **Administrative Law** that governs the actions of administrative agencies of government (federal and state).
- A third source of law is **statutory** or **Statute law** and is the body of laws **created by legislature** or by lesser governing authorities, such as municipalities. Statute law is the statutes and/or ordinances created which are not covered under the US constitution.
- The fourth source of American law is determined by what is taken from the Constitution, and the Declaration of Independence, including the Bill of Rights. **Common Law** is based on the notion of how the courts have interpreted the law. Under common law, the facts of a case are determined and evaluated against previous cases that have similar facts to come to a decision by comparison.

The Constitution is the basis of the United States legal system. Constitutions are the basis for government and may restrict or describe the power and procedures of the government to implement new laws and regulations. The Supreme Court is important to defining and interpreting the Constitution. The Constitution itself contains 27 articles and a "mission statement" (the preamble). One of the main purposes of constitutions is to specify relationships of power and arranges the system in which they govern. The Constitution establishes a federal state, as opposed to a unitary state; it identifies the bodies of government coexisting with limited or joint areas of jurisdiction over creating laws, applying laws, and enforcing the same.

Constitutional Law

The most important source of American law comes from **The Constitution** of the United States and **constitutional law**. All other laws and sources of law fall under constitutional law and all other laws are inferior to constitutional law. The other legal systems are statute law, administrative law and common law. Together these four primary sources are the foundation of American law as well as contributing to the creation of the United States of America, as is witnessed through history.

Constitutional laws are the most important laws and were **created by the founding fathers** of America to provide for the government of the United States. The declarations of independence along with the bill of rights outline the rights and the responsibilities of the country's citizens. Constitutional Law is based on federal or state constitutions, the official document that describes wide-ranging powers.

The foundation of Constitutional law comes from the '**Declaration of Independence**' that was approved and accepted on July 4, 1776, with the purpose of declaring that the Thirteen Colonies in North America were to be "*Free and Independent States*," free from the laws of Britain, and it established new laws for their new country. Historically, this is the basis for the American legal system of today. The Declaration of Independence was mainly written by Thomas Jefferson, with help from John Adams and Benjamin Franklin. There were a total of 56 signers to the Declaration of Independence. The first and most famous signature was that of John Hancock, who was President of the Continental Congress. John Adams (future second President) and Thomas Jefferson (future third President) both signed, as well.

The success of the American Revolution presented Americans with the chance to turn their ideas into legal form, and to solve some of their injustices through **state constitutions**. Congress had passed a resolution in May 1776, which directed the colonies to outline new governments "*such as shall best conduce to the happiness and safety of their constituent.*" The first goal of the creators of state constitutions was to protect the "*unalienable rights*" which already had been defiled and became the primary reason that the earlier colonies had turned away from Britain. Each state constitution starts with a declaration.

THE DECLARATION OF INDEPENDENCE

The Declaration of Independence is the chief document in American law.
With the Declaration of Independence in 1776, the former colonies gained full and complete control over the distribution of authority to create and enforce public and private laws.

Originally given the title "The unanimous Declaration of the thirteen United States of America," it described the reasons for separation from British law. In the beginning, American public opinion was totally divided over the issue. After its acceptance the Declaration of Independence was seen mainly as a statement of separation from Britain and not as the valued political document it is now.

The Bills Of Rights, which make up the first ten amendments of the constitution, were added to the constitutional laws, in order to limit the power of the government and further protect the rights of Americans and visitors to the United States. The Bill of Rights determines that the liberties of the country as a nation can only be protected by its citizens who value the nation's rights and liberties and will enthusiastically protect them.

The Preamble to the United States Constitution introduces the constitution and summarizes its purpose.

The Bill of Rights are the first ten amendments of the Constitution of The United States and can be summarized as follows:

Amendment I:	Freedom of religion, assembly, speech, press and freedom to petition.
Amendment II:	The right to keep and bear arms.
Amendment III:	No quartering of soldiers.
Amendment IV:	Freedom from unreasonable searches and seizures.
Amendment V:	The right to due process of law, freedom from self-incrimination, freedom from double jeopardy.
Amendment VI:	The right to a speedy and public trial.
Amendment VII:	The right to trial by jury.
Amendment VIII:	Freedom from excessive bail, cruel and unusual punishments.
Amendment IX:	Other rights of the people.
Amendment X:	Powers reserved for the states.

ADMINISTRATIVE LAW

The second source of American law is **Administrative law**. Administrative law presides over and governs the procedures of administrative agencies of both federal and state governments. Such agencies are given power by Congress, or state legislature. Administrative agencies are usually formed to protect the public's interests. Government agency activities can include law making and adjudication as well as enforcement.

Administration law regulates such things as immigration, international trading, the environment, and taxation.

Administrative law is broken down into many parts, such as administrative rules, procedures and regulations for government agencies, and enforcement powers of these government agencies. In a wide sense, administrative law is for those parts of government that are neither governed by legislature or the courts. The bodies, called *administrative agencies*, are usually found within the executive branch of government and are generally assigned the day-to-day details of governing. Agencies are developed and given particular tasks from legislature. The agencies then complete these everyday jobs by coming to a variety of decisions and by supervising various actions

Administrative laws are the laws governing the power and actions of administrative agencies. In America, federal and state governments uphold a *tripartite* balance of powers (a three-branch government, which includes legislature, executive, judiciary). Administrative law is mainly responsible to allocate powers to agencies (by Congress) or to secure those powers (by executive agencies) with judicial checks on their procedures. Administrative agencies are developed under constitutional provisions by statute or by executive order approved by statute. The use of administrative agencies in the United States began in 1789, when legislation initially granted them the management of customs laws and created their guidelines for ships and other oceangoing vessels, and pensions to veterans. Towards the end of the nineteenth century, due to growing public transportation and public utilities, agencies began to play an important role in American life. The Interstate Commerce Act and organization of the Interstate Commerce Commission in 1887 was the beginning of more modern administrative laws in the United States.

Administrative laws are laws **created by Congress or state legislature (executive branch)** *to provide the rules and regulations of government agencies. These laws are applied at a federal, state, and local level.*

STATUTE LAW

A third source of law is **statutory** or **statute law** and is the body of laws **created by legislature** or by lesser governing authorities, such as municipalities. The fifty states have separate power and each state has individual state constitutions and governments. They maintain special power to make laws regarding anything that is not covered by the federal Constitution, or by the federal Senate or statutes.

All states began from British common law as the base for their law, except Louisiana. Louisiana law has followed the French Napoleonic Code. Time has created a huge change in the diversity of the laws of states. State courts have extended and built upon the old common law rules in different directions and state legislatures have passed various statutes to override many judge-made rules.

Statutory laws are laws **created by legislature (the Legislative branch)**. Statute laws are the statutes or ordinances that are not covered by the constitution or by constitutional laws and are applied and passed on the federal, state, or local levels.

The clearest sources of American law are the statutes approved by Congress, as added to by administrative regulations. From time to time these statutes plainly distinguish the limitations of legal and illegal actions but no government can publicize a sufficient amount of law to cover every possible situation. Another body of legal doctrine and standards helps solve these issues, called **Common law**.

COMMON LAW

The fourth source of American law is most portrayed in the Constitution, and in the Declaration of Independence, including the Bill of Rights. **Common law** (also called *case law*) got its start in the 13th century. *Common Law* is based on the notion of how the courts have interpreted the law. Under common law, the facts of a case are determined by judges and evaluated against previous cases that have similar facts to come to a decision by comparison. Common law is applied mainly on a state level.

For laws to be effective in regulating and predicting conduct, they must be consistent. The need for such consistency led judges to adopt two principles that govern common law: ***precedent*** *and **stare decisis*** were created to set up uniform rules that apply to all of the country.

Common Law was created throughout the centuries to protect the rights of individuals to their property and to restrict the property to be taken away by the government without due process of law. American common law got its start from English common law. English common law developed because there was no other source of law available, without an available constitution. American Common Law was developed throughout the years in many thousands of case decisions and resulting trials in which the Common Law jury represented the judges, and they used the authority to hear and make a decision on questions of laws and facts. American Common Law focuses on legal relationships and their powers and responsibility, as well as actions. American Common Law was accepted by the Founding Fathers and is the foundation of all law in America in the present day. Common Law accepts that the Power of Government is a responsibility of the common people and not in a select few leaders. Admiralty Laws, also called laws of contract or equity law, take this power from the people and give the power to federal and state governments. The **judge** in a Court of Common Law is a neutral arbitrator of disputes, and is bound to protect the Rights of the parties to the disagreement, or the judge will lose what authority he had. It is the **jury** who will decide if the details of the case are valid. The jury also decides if the law applies or if it is proper for the case.

Common law crimes and the common law legal tradition were given to the North American colonies from English common laws, and presently they shape the beginning of a large amount of statutory and case law in America. The influence of *common law* on present-day *criminal law* is so vast that it is sometimes referred to as **the primary source** of modern criminal law.

When no statute or constitutional conditions exist, federal and state courts often turn to the common law and to a collection of previous judicial decisions, traditions, and ethics that got their start centuries ago in England and continue to expand today. Common law still holds a crucial role in contract disputes, in many states, as state legislatures have not found a way to approve statutes that cover all possible contract conditions.

Common law is applied mainly on a state level **(the Judicial branch)**. Common laws were created to protect the rights of individuals to property. American common law is created by judges.

DEMOCRACY

Democracy plays a crucial role in freedom and liberty. The dictionary defines democracy as "government by the people in which the supreme power is vested in the people and exercised directly by them or by their elected agents under a free electoral system." Abraham Lincoln explained democracy as "a government of the people, by the people, and for the people."

To understand the deeper meaning of democracy in America one should begin by understanding the notion that democracy is a set of practices and procedures that have been created throughout our long American history.

There are two fundamental categories of democracy:

Direct democracy (*pure democracy*), in which all citizens play a part in making public decisions. (This system is only realistic within small communities.)

Representative democracy (*the most familiar form of democracy*), in which the citizens elect officials to make political decisions, govern programs for the best interests of the public, and create laws. The elected officials are bound to the will of the citizens.

Federalism

Federalism is the division of responsibilities and duties between the federal government and separate state governments. The Constitution permits the federal government specific powers; other authorities not exclusively delegated to federal government are given to the state governments' authority. This distribution of power is necessary and has had an important effect on the process if laws in America.

Federal authority controls the laws of pensions, patents, profit sharing, and labor.

State authority controls the laws of contracts, business association, and trade secrets within each state.

Concurrent authority controls security law, tax law, and employment law, coexisting between national and state authority.

Types of Law

Criminal law: the rules and statutes that characterize acts which are prohibited by the government due to their threat or harm to public safety and wellbeing; these rules and statutes create necessary penalties to be obligatory for such acts.

Civil law: the rules that outline private rights and remedies, and oversee disagreements and disputes between two or more individuals.

Substantive law: makes, describes, and controls rights, such as: the law of contracts, TORTS, and real property; the important essence of rights under law.

Procedural law: Also known as *adjective law*, it is the laws which govern the functions of courts and the manner by which both the state and the individual (or groups) impose their rights in the courts.

Jurisdiction

Jurisdiction is the power of a state concerning property, persons, and circumstances within its area. This power may be enforced through legislative, executive, or judicial actions.

For a court to have jurisdiction, it must have both *subject matter jurisdiction* and *personal jurisdiction*.

Subject Matter Jurisdiction is the power over the claim being made. **Personal Jurisdiction** is having the power over the person(s) involved in the claim.

Legal action can begin in any place where the subject or person involved in the lawsuit is situated. **Local actions** are legal actions that can be brought only in the county (or district) where the subject or person involved in the case is situated.

Venue is the county (or region) inside a state where the court case is being tried. The venue of a case is made by statute, but occasionally it can transfer to another area (as when trying a high profile case).

All states have two separate courts: state and federal. The majority of cases are brought to state courts.

A **writ of certiorari** comes from the Latin meaning "to be more fully informed." This is the process by which a higher court can review decisions and cases that took place in a lower court. For example, the Supreme Court handpicks most of its cases and uses a writ of certiorari to have the lower courts send the information to them for the case. Through a writ of certiorari the higher court can review the decision for an irregularities or possible mistakes made.

Types of Courts

Federal courts have authority over cases that involve federal statutes, constitutional questions, and certain other types of cases. Appeals on constitutional questions and other major cases are heard by the Supreme Court, but only if that court will agree to hear the case.

STATE COURTS

Each state has local trial courts, which include courts for misdemeanors and smaller demand civil actions (*usually called* **municipal court**) and then courts in each county (*usually called* **District or County courts**) to hear felonies, divorces and major lawsuits. The **State Supreme Court** is the highest state court. Various states have **specialty courts**, most commonly, **family court**. **Small claims courts** are an addition of the lowest courts handling lesser arguments and disputes and have no legal representation with informal trials supervised by a judge or by lawyers.

- **Trial court:** *(court of first instance)* is the court in where nearly all civil and criminal cases initiate.
- **Appellate court:** court with the authority to hear an appeal of a trial court or other lower cases.
- **Supreme court:** *(court of last resort)* the highest level of court whose decisions (rulings) cannot be disputed. The Supreme Court can also act as the *judge, jury, and the court* in a trial.

Judges

Judges work for the state. Although they work for the state, they are not law enforcement officers. Judges do not have the power to arrest people and it is not *their* responsibility to attempt to prove guilt. The responsibility of the judge is to ensure that the laws of court procedures are maintained from all sides.

The judge is an officer with the authority to supervise a court, try lawsuits and make legal decisions (**rulings**). Judges of courts win their office through elections, or by a type of judicial selection method. Federal judges are selected by the President of the U.S. along with agreement by the U.S. Senate.

The **judge** oversees the courtroom. The judge will instruct the jury on the rules of law that govern the case. For non-jury cases, the judge will determine the facts and deliver a judgment.

The **court clerk** or often the bailiff generally will administer an oath to jurors and witnesses. The **bailiff** maintains order in the courtroom and is in control of the jury, as ordered by the judge.

The **court reporter** accounts for **everything** that is said during the official proceedings to include objections of attorneys and witness testimony. In some jurisdictions and cases, audio or video recording are also made.

Juries

Juries are a group of citizens from within the community who are called upon to determine the facts of a case.

The jury will hear testimonies and listen to evidence throughout the course of a trial. Then they will determine what facts the evidence has proven, and come to a conclusion (reach a **verdict**) from those facts.

The responsibility of the judge is to determine which evidence the jury can consider. The jury is to find the facts only from the evidence that is admissible. The judge also supervises and instructs the jury regarding the legal doctrine and rules for examining the facts. If the jury determines that the accused party is guilty or liable, it is the responsibility of the judge to deliver the sentence.

Few lawsuits ever go through the full array of procedures and end with a trial. Most civil cases are completed by a mutual agreement. A conflict can often be settled before a suit is even filed. After a suit is filed, it can be settled out of court (before the trial begins), throughout the trial, or even after a verdict is rendered. An agreement or settlement doesn't generally affirm that one was right or wrong within the case, and it does not have to resolve the full case. Part of a case can be settled, with the remaining disagreements left to be determined by the judge or jury.

Criminal cases are not settled by the parties involved in the same way civil cases are. Still, not every case goes to trial. The prosecutor can come to a decision to dismiss and stop prosecuting a case. The accused (defendant) may choose to plead guilty, possibly a result of bargaining and negotiating with the prosecutor that result in dismissing some of the charges.

All legal cases are broken down into two categories: civil and criminal.

Civil cases entail a disagreement or **conflict between two or more people** or entities such as businesses. A civil case usually begins when a person or business establishes that a problem cannot be resolved unless the court gets involved.

Civil suits start when one of the parties involved files a complaint with the court. The *plaintiff* or *petitioner* is the party who is filing the lawsuit. The person or business the case is filed against is the *defendant* or *respondent*.

Divorces, child custody and support entail a great number of civil cases.

Criminal cases are suits initiated by a prosecutor working for the government (federal, state or local) that accuse a person with a criminal act.

The most severe crimes are labeled as **felonies**, the punishment on conviction of a felony crime is imprisonment for *at least* a year. **Misdemeanors** are less severe crimes; punishment is most often imprisonment of *up to* one year, or less. **Petty misdemeanors** most often involve a punishment of a fine without imprisonment.

Mistrials are trials that are not concluded properly. They are canceled and said to be invalid before a verdict is rendered by a jury or the judge delivers her decision in a trial without a jury present.

Mistrials can happen for various reasons:

- The jury is not able to reach a unanimous agreement to render their verdict (deadlocked)
- Death of an attorney or a juror
- An error prejudicial or unfair to the defendant

An **appeal** is a written request to a higher level court to change or overturn the decision (judgment) of a court.

Examination

Lawyers for the plaintiff or the petitioner start presenting evidence by calling witnesses. The questions they ask witnesses are called the **direct examination**. Direct examination can produce circumstantial and direct evidence. In general witnesses are not permitted to offer their opinion unless they are experts in areas that are relevant to the case, making them **expert witnesses**.

When the lawyer for the plaintiff or the petitioner is done questioning a witness, the lawyer for the defendant or respondent will also ask questions of the witness (called cross-examination). **Cross-examination** is usually restricted to asking questions about issues that were raised through the direct examination. During cross-examination, the lawyer can try to question the witness's capacity to recognize or recall the evidence. Witnesses can be asked if they have ever been convicted of a crime concerning dishonesty since this is applicable to establishing their credibility. Opposing lawyers can **object** to some questions during cross-examination if the questions go against the laws of the state regarding evidence or if the questions pertain to issues that were not raised during direct examination.

The **closing arguments** of the lawyers talk about the evidence and conclusions that were drawn during examination. The lawyers cannot discuss evidence that was not previously presented through the examination and/or testimony.

The lawyer for the plaintiff more often than not presents his closing argument first. After the plaintiff's lawyer has made his case and presented his closing argument, the defense will present his closing arguments. The defense lawyer usually comments on and discusses statements that were made in the plaintiff's closing argument, and summarizes the facts that will present his side in the best way to win the favor of the jury.

Due Process of Law

The law that says the government must allow for the complete legal rights of a person, and not only part of those rights, is known as **due process of law**. The fifth amendment of the constitution protects this right to due process and states that due process must be followed and accepted within the legal system of America. The fourteenth amendment follows along with the Fifth Amendment in relation to due process of law.

Assault and Battery

Assault and battery are two of the most common crimes that occur. They are distinct but are often seen together. Assault involves the threat of pain or violence. In order for an act to qualify as an assault, three basic conditions must be met. First, there must be an immediate threat of physical violence; second, the victim must have a reasonable apprehension; third, the act must be intentional. In other words, if an individual was not aware of any potential harm, such as if they were hit from behind, it is technically not assault. Also, simply making threats does not qualify as an assault unless the victim has a reasonable justification for feeling immediately threatened – such as if the threats are made while the person waves a knife or advances to strike.

Battery is the actual act of committing violence. Battery need not be restricted to simply physically injuring another individual, but extends to any action which is involves the use of force on another individual which results in physical harm or unwanted touching. As with assault, that the act was intentional is also a requirement of a battery charge. Any intentional, forceful contact with another individual is battery, regardless of the severity or whether injury was caused.

Contracts

Contracts come into being to make sure everybody involved with a deal of any kind keeps his word. Contracts are promises that are binding and enforced by the law. Whether it's a contract between two people or contracts between business deals, contracts exist to keep us honest and to ensure agreed-to promises are kept. Contracts are one of the most extensive fields of the law and it's safe to say that contracts are used more now than ever before with the promise of continued growth. Contracts deal with all of business negotiations as well as dealings in domestic life. The **formation** of a contract is when two or more people agree to behave in a specific manner. Normally, there is a mutuality of consideration for an agreement to be enforceable. The parties involved in a contract also have to be competent. A contract with a person who has been determined as insane is likely to be declared void. Persons suffering with a disability, like intoxication from alcohol or drugs, will void a contract too. All parties involved must both acquire a benefit and suffer a detriment. In contract law, the duties and obligation of the parties are created by the parties themselves and appear in the form of a contract. If one violates his/her obligation to the contract, the party involved can turn around and sue the offending violator. For a contract to be legally binding, a promise must be exchanged for adequate consideration. **Adequate consideration** is a benefit or detriment the party receives that reasonably and fairly induces them to make the promise/contract. However, gifts are not considered enforceable by contract because, due to the personal satisfaction the grantor promises, his or her intent of the promise cannot be truly known. Contracts are mainly governed by state statutory and judge-made law and private law. Private law principally includes the terms of the agreement between the parties who are exchanging promises to each other. This private law can override many of the rules otherwise established by state law. Statutory law may require some contracts be put in writing and executed with particular formalities. If not, the parties may enter into a binding agreement without signing a formal written document.

The Six Elements of a Contract

A contract is defined as a legally binding agreement *written*, or *verbal*, and in some cases *implied*, between *two or more capable parties*, in exchange for goods or services. The parties come to the agreement after careful and adequate consideration to perform (or in many cases, to refrain from) service(s).

A contract is **valid** when specific elements exist. There must be *intention*, and it must be communicated. When one party makes an offer and the other party accepts the offer including its terms and conditions and when a thing of value has been exchanged (i.e., money, goods, or a *promise*), this constitutes a valid contract. The contract forms a commitment to do (or not do) a thing of value.

There are six elements of a contract that help to conclude if it meets legal criteria to be considered a *valid* contract, and they are:

1) **Offer:** the proposal or expression of intentions, having certain and definite terms and conditions, communicated directly between both parties.
2) **Acceptance:** when the party who is offered the exchange agrees to the definite and certain terms and willingly accepts the offer.
3) **Capacity:** both parties must have the ability to enter into the contract and to comprehend the terms of the contract. (Excluded from a valid contract are minors, intoxicated persons, the mentally impaired, aliens, and convicts.)
4) **Consideration:** the exchange of *benefits* and *detriments* by the parties involved in the contract
5) **Mutual agreement:** the shared comprehension of intentions between both parties, mutual agreement occurs after an offer has been accepted.
6) **Legality:** a contract can not contain illegal subject matter.

WHAT MAKES A CONTRACT VALID?

Normal, everyday English is best to convey written agreements. For most contracts to be lawfully valid and legally binding only two elements are actually required:

1. The *offer* has been made and the offer, along with its terms and conditions, has been accepted, resulting in both parties making a mutual agreement. (This will involve *consideration* of the agreement which will lead to the next element; the exchange.)
2. An *exchange* (money, goods or promise) has taken place for another thing of value.

Often, the agreement does not necessarily need to be documented or in writing. However, specific states do require an agreement covering a one year span of time to include a written contract agreement (i.e., real estate agreements). Although it is sensible to document all business agreements using a written contract, it is also wise to check your state laws before entering into any agreement devoid of a contract.

Contracts are also classified by the manner in which they are formed; there are **express** contracts and **implied** contracts.

Express contracts are those whose terms are stated by the parties at the time of drawing up the contract. Implied contracts are those where there is an implied agreement, although not in writing. For example: when you go to a restaurant to eat, you know that you're expected to pay at the end of the meal, although it's not written anywhere that this is the contract you have made.

An **agreement** is the union of two or more persons with a common goal in mind, by expression of will, word or conduct, which will make a legal relationship. It is an act in law where two or more persons declare their consent as to any act or thing to be done or not done by one or more of those persons. Such declarations can take place either by (A) the concurrence of the parties in a spoken or written form of words as expressing their common intention, or (B) by an offer made by some or one of the persons and accepted by the others. Because the intention of will can only be known by expression of words or conduct, the law imputes to each of the parties a state of mind or intention corresponding to the natural and reasonable meaning of his words and conduct no matter what may have been a person's real state of mind or secret intention. The intention must also be with reference to the creation of legal relations and contemplate legal consequences affecting the parties themselves. Agreements are the essential elements of a true contract.

A **consideration** of a contract is the inducement, price or motive that causes a party to enter into an agreement or contract. With that said, just because a promise has been made does not meant the promise can or will be enforced. Back in the days of Roman law, a promise was not enforceable unless there was a reason for making a promise in the first place. In the beginning of common law in England, not only did one need a good reason for enforcing informal promises but an agreed-upon exchange that would benefit the promisor also had to be included in order for the promise to happen. Through the years, these reasons came to be known as "consideration" and today, no promise is to be enforced without consideration. Most consideration are defined as value, most likely money, which is to be exchanged in return for a promise. An example would be the promise to sell something upon the receipt of payment. Consideration are broken down into two parts.

(1) Something of legal value must be given in exchange for the promise.
(2) There must be a bargained-for exchange.

This bargained-for exchange has to be something of legal value and can consist of a return promise. If the promise is a performance, this can be an act (other than a promise), a forbearance (refraining from action), or the creation, modification or destruction of a legal relation.

For example: Mom wants her son to wash her car, and she offers him $20.00 to do so. The act of washing the car is the consideration that creates the contract and Mom's obligation to pay her son $20.00.

In order for a binding contract to be made, consideration has to be **legally sufficient** and to be legally sufficient, the consideration for a promise must be either legally detrimental to the person receiving the promise or legally beneficial to the person making the promise. A legal detriment is not synonymous with economic detriment because a person can incur legal detriment in either of two ways: (1) by doing or promising to do something that he or she had no prior legal duty to do or (2) by refraining from or promising to refrain from doing something that he or she had no prior legal duty to refrain from doing.

Adequacy of consideration refers to the fairness of the bargain in a contract. If the bargain is fair, a court will not question the adequacy of consideration as long as it's legally sufficient. The freedom of contract doctrine states that parties are free to bargain whatever they want because while not every contract is going to be good, not every person is going to sue because of a bad contract. If this was true, the courts could not handle the overload of frivolous suits. In extreme cases, the court may consider the adequacy of consideration in terms of worth because an inadequate consideration may indicate fraud duress, undue influence or even a lack of bargained-for exchange. It could also show the parties' incompetence and will want to look for determining factors such as if someone was too intoxicated or even too young to legally make a contract. For example, say Carl sold his house for $50,000 but it was worth over $100,000. This would make the court suspicious of why he sold it for so cheap. Was he under duress? Why was he in such a hurry to sell? When it comes to equity suits, courts will look more closely into the adequacy of consideration. In an equity suit, defendants will have the burden of showing the transaction was not under duress.

Contracts that lack consideration refer to when people make mistakes. Sometimes one or both parties in a contract believe they have exchanged consideration when they have not. The following are some reasons why promises or actions do not qualify as contractual consideration.

Some consideration can be declared unnecessary by statute. Contracts of record such as judgments, formal bonds, money pledges and indemnity bonds do not need to be supported by a consideration because they are binding by virtue of the fact that they are founded upon the authority and the sanction of a court of competent jurisdiction.

Preexisting duty is a promise to do what one person already has a legal duty to do; however, it does not constitute legally sufficient consideration because no legal detriment has happened. For example: A cop cannot collect a bounty for catching a criminal because he already has the legal duty to capture criminals. If a party is already bound by contract to perform a certain duty, which duty cannot serve as a consideration for a second contract. For example, a contractor is under contract to build an office building. Two months later he demands more money or he will not complete the project. The owner has no one else to finish building so he pays the contractor. This agreement is not enforceable because it is not supported legally by sufficient consideration since the contractor was already in a preexisting contract to complete the building in the first place.

UNFORESEEN DIFFICULTIES

Preexisting duty is meant to prevent extortion. But as we all know, things happen, even to honest contractors. For example, a contractor has contracted with a land owner to build a building, but then runs into difficulties that were not foreseen when the contract was being put together. The courts may allow exceptions to the preexisting duty rule if the landowner agrees to pay extra compensation to the contractor for the unforeseen difficulties.

RESCISSION AND NEW CONTRACT

Rescission is defined as the unmaking of a contract so as to return the parties to the positions they occupied before the contract was made. The law recognizes that two parties can mutually agree to rescind their contract still to be carried out.

Past consideration are promises made in return for actions or events that have already taken place and are unenforceable because the element of bargained-for exchange is missing. This means that you can bargain for something in the future or taking place now but you cannot bargain for something that has already happened. Past consideration is not consideration.

Third Party Contracts

When a contract involves a **third party**, usually two people are involved in the contract while the third person makes the promise to pay either party to perform the contract. Not all third party contracts have enforceable contract rights and the only way to make sure they get these rights is to make sure he or she is the intended beneficiary within the contract. In order to qualify as intended beneficiary, he or she must meet two requirements. (1) the third party must show that recognition of a right to performance by the beneficiary is appropriate to effectuate the intention of the parties and (2) the performance of the promise will satisfy an obligation of the promise to pay money to the beneficiary or the circumstances indicate that the promise intends to give the beneficiary the benefit of the promised performance.

Obligations

An **obligation** is a requirement and duty to do what is imposed by law, promise, or contract. A better way to describe an obligation is to call it a duty, meaning it is a tie that binds us to pay or to do something agreeable to the laws and customs of the country in which the obligation is made. The term obligation also means that although a civil obligation is to be a bond that contains a penalty, a condition annexed for the payment of money, performance of covenants or the like, the instrument or writing by which the contract is made contains a penalty, with a condition annexed for the payment of money, performance of covenants or the like, if someone chooses to break their obligation. An obligation also means a writing by which the contract is witnessed.

Obligations are separated into two distinctions, **imperfect obligations and perfect obligations**. A **perfect obligation** gives the right to one person and requires the other to give him something or not to do something. These obligations are natural, moral or civil.

Imperfect obligations are those which are not binding on the parties as between two people, and those for which non-performance makes the party accountable to God only, such as charity or gratitude. In this sense an obligation is a mere duty.

Natural obligations or moral obligations cannot be enforced by actions but a person can still be obliged to do what was first intended, in agreement with natural justice. If an action is closed because of a restriction or limit, there is no more natural obligation. Natural obligations cannot be enforced by law but they can have the following effect, there can be no lawsuit to recover back what has been paid or given in compliance with a natural obligation. A natural obligation can be enough relevance in assessing a new contract.

There are many different types of obligations when it comes to contracts. Civil obligations are those that are binding an operation in law and give the other person the right to take things to court. There are many different names for civil obligations and they are divided into many terms like pure and conditional, principal and accessory, primitive and secondary, divisible and indivisible, in other words, for every positive civil obligation there's a negative obligation.

Implied obligations are those that come to be with an action that has been set in motion. For example: If I come over and fix something for you, like an oven or washing machine, and you use it to benefit you and your family, under law you are then obligated to pay me the value of the job. Whether you do it or not is up to you, as implied obligations are hard to enforce.

Other obligations:

(1) Pure and simple obligations are ineffective because there are either no conditions holding to the contract or the obligation has already been fulfilled.

(2) Conditional obligations can be suspended if the condition has not been accomplished or the deal falls through.

(3) Primitive obligations (principal obligations) are those that are contracted with a design that has to be fulfilled.

(4) Secondary obligations are different because they back up primitive obligations. If the first one can't be done then the secondary obligation will be.

(5) Accessory obligations are dependent on principal obligations.

(6) Absolute obligations don't give the obligor much of a choice, he or she has to fulfill an absolute obligation, one way or another. If the person under the obligation for some reason cannot give what was first promised, then he/she has to give up something else of the same value.

Obligations become very personal when a person binds him or herself to do a certain thing. For example: an individual promises to pay another a certain amount of money every month until the time to end the payments is specified. If not specified, then at the time of the promisor's death, the contract ends unless otherwise specified.

There is an obligation to cover just about any contract that comes into being and the list goes on and on, but the list here contains some of the more familiar obligations that one will come across when dealing with contracts.

 Condequentialism

Consequentialism is a philosophy that states that the consequences of an action are the basis of morality. In other words, if an act provides positive results, then the act is morally right. If one action produces more good consequences than another, then it is the more morally correct act. On the other hand, if an action results in bad consequences, then the act is morally wrong. Although this theory is well-intentioned in examining the greatest overall benefit to society, it is also a dangerous method of thinking because it allows for rationalization of actions that would traditionally be considered immoral. For example, consequentialism could be used to justify any number of behaviors such as lying and stealing to achieve a competitive business advantage. Because of this, it is important that a person takes a long-term perspective when using this ethical philosophy.

 Validity of Contracts

In order for a contract to be **valid**, there must be a mutual agreement between two people. The signing of a contract between two people means that both parties agree to certain terms. This keeps both parties honest. For example, a man hires another to paint his house; the painter agrees to paint the house for $400. The painter paints the house and the man is happy with the work and pays the agreed $400.

An older theory of a valid contract was said to be the **meeting of the minds**. There are still some definitions of contract law that start out with "it takes a meeting of the minds to form a contract." This is not considered to be a valid contract since one person could resist a claim of breach by proving although it may have appeared impartially that he or she intended to be bound by the agreement, he never truly intended to be bound. This was not a good validation of a contract since other parties have no means of knowing their counterparts undisclosed intentions or understandings. They can only act upon what a party reveals objectively to be his/her intent.

Voidable Contracts

A **voidable** contract occurs when one of the parties will reject the contract based on legal grounds. The contract will remain valid and enforceable, unless the party, who has ground to reject the contract, will void it. A contract is considered to be *void* (or *voidable*) if any one of the elements are absent or omitted. A void or voidable contract is not legally binding and therefore bears no ground for legal action.

There are three classifications of contracts that can not be legally binding. A contract is 1) **void** if it is based on illegal actions or purposes and contrary to public policy. This contract is not recognized by the courts of law and not enforceable by either party. Contracts with minors can be 2) **voidable**, and a contract is also voidable if a person signs under the influence of alcohol or drugs. Mental weakness, whether it's from an illness, age or any other cause, but does not destroy his or her ability to comprehend the nature and effect of a contract, offers no ground for him or her not entering a contract if there is no evidence in showing any fraud, duress or undue influence. The law states that even if a person does not have the mental facilities of a regular person, he or she may still enter into a contract and there will be no grounds to make the contract voidable. As long as a person understands what's going on, his or her acts will be valid. If a contract 3) **violates** the Statute of Frauds, it's considered **unenforceable**. An example of an unenforceable contract would be an oral contract for the sale of a car for $1200. In the U.S. anything sold for over $500 must be made in writing for it to be enforceable.

Under traditional contract law, minors are not considered capable to enter into a contract because they lack the legal capacity to do so. In other words, they aren't fully responsible for their choices and can't be held accountable for them. Because of this lack of capacity in making agreements, a minor can legally revoke any contracts that they enter into at any time before reaching the age of adulthood (or within a reasonable amount of time before adulthood). There are very few exceptions to this rule, but one includes contracts for the necessaries of life. If a minor's caregivers are not adequately providing them with the necessities of life – including food, shelter, and clothing – then contracts that they enter into to obtain these necessities are binding. This exception was put into place to avoid abuse of the law by parents.

Duress

Duress is the unlawful coercion used to make another person act or not to act in a manner they normally would not choose. The threatening of violence toward another person to make him/her enter into a contract or to release one constitutes duress. In order to claim duress as a defense, a person has to show that he or she was forced into an agreement to the contract by a serious threat of unlawful or wrongful action, and that he/she had no other choice but to sign the contract. Blackmail is a good example of duress.

Consideration

A contract is unenforceable and not binding unless both parties will exchange something of value (money, goods or a promise) to complete the contract. This exchange is the contract consideration. What represents an exchange and equals proper consideration is determined by the legal rules concerning the exchange.

Consideration is some profit or benefit given to the one party, with responsibility or detriment to the other. The thing of value that is being exchanged (consideration) is often a promise to do a job or a promise to pay a fee for a work. A moral responsibility to pay a debt or carry out a duty is adequate consideration for an *express promise*, while no legal responsibility was created at the time of making the express promise.

There are three core purposes for the consideration requirement.

- *Cautionary requirement* – careful thought rather than a spontaneous promise.
- *Evidentiary requirement* – negotiating requirement which increases chances that the parties will clearly define and record the terms
- *Channeling requirement* – both parties are more likely to clearly specify their needs when they are forced to negotiate and discuss them. Clearly defines gifts, unclear promises and unsolicited rewards. Each of these can ensure that contracts are clearly understood by the involved parties and are not made spontaneously or in error.

In a few states, a gratuitous promise can be lawfully enforceable if the party who has made the promise was dependant upon the promise, although, many states no longer require consideration for some promises. If one party makes a promise and the other party makes no offer for anything in exchange for that promise, the promise is not legally binding. This is called a "gratuitous promise."

Lack of consideration is seldom a dilemma for promises made in business interactions. In most business contracts, there is mutual consideration. Consideration is lawfully enforceable and binding when there is enough to support the contract or render the contract void. If the performance is absolutely not achievable the consideration is then also deemed to be lawfully void and consequently unenforceable.

Mutual Agreement

Agreement involves the discussions of the offer. During the discussions the negotiating process usually begins. And since the negotiation is not the actual contract, the law needs to be able to clearly understand when the negotiation process has ended and when the involved parties have reached mutual agreement. The legal approach to the answer of when the parties have reached mutual agreement is to verify if they have accomplished the initial steps of *offer and acceptance*. The first step to the formation of a contract is the offer, followed by acceptance of the offer. When one party makes an offer, upon the acceptance of the offer from the other party, a legal contract is formed. The offer should present what you are offering in detail, along with exactly what you expect to receive in return. The contract offer should describe the goods or services in specific and definite terms, meaning the terms and conditions should be clearly defined.

Before presenting an offer to another party you will need to outline the contract. You could find some sample contracts online or in books. Many standard contract agreements can be downloaded online for a fee. You can use a contract template and enter the detailed terms you choose, or you can draft a completely original contract, yourself.

You should outline the terms of the contract before creating the contract. Describe what you want as detailed as possible; also tell what you are offering in exchange, clearly. Avoid any confusion by using short and direct sentences. This will make the contract much easier to understand, for both parties. Categorize headings to permit ease for moving through the contract. Throughout the body of the contract, along with clearly defined terms, discuss any possible situations that may surface in the future of the contract, such as how to solve specific issues that may possibly arise, and who will be responsible, in the event of a breach of contract, etc. Allow for appropriate space on the final page for both parties' signatures, including addresses, phone numbers and attorney information, if applicable.

Generally, an offer is considered to be open for a reasonable amount of time if the contract does not specifically state an expiration date. Reasonable time depends largely upon the situation. The inclusion of an expiration date in the contract will help to avoid any future confusion regarding the expiration of the offer. Until the offer is accepted, it can be revoked. Revoking the offer must occur prior to its acceptance taking place. After the acceptance is made, the contract is formed and lawfully enforceable and binding. The only time an offer is not binding after the acceptance is if the expiration date is detailed within the contract itself and the acceptance is made after the expiration date. The one who made the offer (called the *offeror*) can not revoke the offer until the contract has expired.

Frequently, when an offer has been made, negotiations will begin. A counteroffer occurs when a party replies to an offer with a different offer. Now the responsibility of acceptance moves to the original offeror. The original offer will be formed only if the acceptance is made and the party agrees to accept the original terms and conditions. Revoking an offer as well as amending the offer or presenting a counteroffer, may lead to misunderstandings and/or disagreements. Despite the delay, these are frequent conditions occurring in many business transactions. The contractual steps of offer and acceptance can become quite complicated, although they would seem to be rather simple.

Acceptance

There are generally three types of acceptance in contract law. These include:

1. **Implied acceptance:** not stated clearly but confirmed by actions signifying a person's agreement to the offer.

2. **Express acceptance:** when a person openly agrees to the offer, without doubt as to the acceptance.
3. **Conditional** (*often referred to as qualified*) **acceptance:** a person who was presented with the offer states to the offeror that they are accepting the agreement to the offer on the condition that changes are made in the terms or that some a specific event takes place.

This acceptance will be known as a counteroffer and must be accepted by the original offeror before the contract can be formed and legally binding.

Acceptance of an offer includes various important details the one being presented with the offer should carefully consider prior to acceptance:

- *Time of acceptance*: if the terms of the offer directly state that an action must be taken within a limited amount of time or before a stated expiration time, the offer must meet those time restrictions in order to form a binding contract.
- *Location of acceptance*: Location of where the contract was formed and where it was accepted will determine which laws (state, federal, or municipality) will govern the contract.
- *When the acceptance takes place*: more often than not acceptance takes place when it is stated to the offeror, when the offeror receives the statement (or message) of acceptance.

Capacity

Concerning the capacity to contract, minors (under the age of 18, in most states) and the mentally incompetent fall short of the *legal* capacity to enter into legally binding contracts. Generally all others are assumed to have full power to legally bind them and lawfully enter into contracts. Whether the party understood the nature and results or consequences of the contract is usually determined to test mental capacity.

Exempt from entering a binding or enforceable contract are minors under the minimum age limit, anyone who is mentally unsound, those who are intoxicated, aliens and convicts. However, evidence must prove that the parties are in fact incompetent and did not know what they were doing at the time of the agreement. All others are assumed to have mental capacity to be bound by legal contracts.

Basically, a party may be an individual, or a group of people, or an entity such as a corporation. The parties must have the *legal capacity* to enter into the contract. Parties who are found to be incompetent due to physical or mental illness are lacking in capacity to contract. Minors **may** enter into contracts. However, contracts involving a minor are *voidable*. An unfulfilled contract which involves a minor may be affirmed or disaffirmed when the minor reaches the age of maturity (18 in most states), or legally becomes an adult, through emancipation. Legal capacity to agree of a minor is the source of many debates. A contract formed with a minor is voidable by the minor party but not voidable by the adult party.

The law presumes that each person has a capacity to contract. Incapacity must be proven by the one claiming the incapacity.

Legality

A contract cannot violate "public policy" if it is to be enforceable. If the issue of a contract is illegal, it violates the law and therefore it does not constitute a legally binding and enforceable contract.

Public policy can change. Many states will not enforce gambling debts, though many states have allowed gambling within their jurisdictions, and gambling debts incurred from legal businesses are now usually enforceable.

Joint Obligations

Joint obligations are contracts where even if there are two or more individuals within the contract, it separates them in liability and each person is only responsible for their part of the contract.

Termination of an Offer

If an offer to a contract is withdrawn before acceptance, there is no contract; this is known as **termination of an offer**. There are different forms of termination:

- The party offering may revoke their offer if no consideration has been given.
- The offer may lapse, either after a specified time, or it may become too old.
- An offer may come to an end after a stipulated event occurs or does not occur.

- The offer may lapse on death of one party.
- If the offer is killed by a counteroffer, be careful of the word "counteroffer." This can be a tricky word. The one making the counteroffer may only mean that a request was given for information only, and the original offer may still be good.

There are several terms that come under the termination of an offer when making contracts. One such term is **unilateral mistake** and it deals with the quality of the subject matter and can be a very problematic area. An example of a unilateral mistake would be if one person declares, "I wanted a left-handed, double action, high impact stapler, and what you have delivered is a right-handed, single action, low impact stapler." What was actually negotiated was "a stapler." This is known as a **unilateral mistake**, only one party is mistaken. A **bilateral mistake** is when both parties believe they are getting one thing but are actually getting another.

Mistake as to the identity of a person/party happens when one person believes he/she is dealing with one person, when in actuality they are dealing with another. When the first person finds out there is really no such person, the contract between them can be voided for fraud and not a mistake. If a person assumes a fictitious business name and buys goods from another person who believes they are dealing with someone else, this contract is voidable for fraud and not void for a mistake. Say for example a man named Fred, an infamous money lender, assumed another name like Sam and loaned money to a person at 50% interest. The contract would be voidable for fraud on the assumption that the borrower would not have borrowed the money in the first place had he known he was dealing with Fred.

Mistakes to subject matter can occur as well. This can happen when at the time a contract was made, the subject matter the contract pertained to did not exist anymore, unbeknownst to both parties. This agreement is void.

If the subject matter is a horse that had died, neither part is held responsible. Sometimes a mistake happens when one party is thinking one thing while the other party is thinking another. For example: A person agrees to buy some property from another person. The lot the first person wants to buy is next to the grade school. However, the owner believes the other party wants the lot next to the city park; in this instance, no contract has been made. If another contract is for the sale of pine trees, the buyers wants Florida Pine Trees, and the selling is thinking Georgia Pine Trees, because there is a discrepancy between the notes, this is a mistake preventing the formation of a contract. Another contract for the sale of a cargo is to arrive on the "Titanic" from Greenland, but come to find out there were two ships with the name "Titanic" sailing from the same port at the same time. Because the buyer was thinking of one ship while the seller was thinking of the other, the agreement is void.

Government contracts can be re-written if and when the contracting officer had direct or indirect knowledge that a contractor's bid or proposal contained a clear or clerical or mathematical **error** or misreading of the specifications. This matter was discussed in more detail by the U.S. Courts of Federal Claims and through those discussions the court determined there would be five "elements of proof necessary to establish a unilateral mistake in the context of a government contract." "The contractor must show by clear and convincing evidence that:

- A mistake in fact occurred prior to contract award.
- The mistake was an honest clerical or mathematical error or the misreading of the specifications and not a judgmental error.
- Prior to award the Government knew, or should have known, that a mistake had been made and therefore, should have requested bid verification.
- The Government did not request bid verification or its request for bid verification was inadequate, and
- Proof of the intended bid is established."

Mistakes of Law

Mistakes of law usually arise when the character or the performance of the contract is in question. Contracts dealing in gambling or a contract to commit a crime are specific examples. When the illegality in question is about the character or condition of the contractor, the mistake may be either one of law or one of fact. For example, a contract from a corporation for the purchase of certain types of securities is illegal, not because these securities themselves are illegal, but having these securities in the first place is strictly forbidden. The mistake of the plaintiff selling the bonds may arise either from ignorance of the prohibition—a mistake of law—or ignorance of the extent of the company's holdings—a mistake of fact. In most jurisdictions, money paid under a mistake of law may not be recovered.

When a person draws up a contract with another party who is assuming another identity or business name, the contract can be voidable for fraud because the contract was drawn under false pretenses, the company's assumed name. If the first person finds out about the other party's assumed name, he or she can try to sue for damages.

A **bilateral contract** includes two promises, one by each party to the contract.

A **bilateral mistake** occurs when the parties to a contract are both wrong about the **same** material fact(s) within the contract. There is no *consensus ad idem* (meeting of the minds) and there is no real offer and acceptance. Therefore the contract is considered void.

Unilateral Mistake

Normally, a **unilateral mistake** gives no foundation for avoiding a contract (not entirely voidable, but it can be 'avoided'). A contract containing a typographical error may simply be corrected. A contract may be **avoided** if the mistake in value in the exchange is considerable or if the mistake is caused by or known to the other party. If the mistake is obvious, the contract will be unenforceable, but if it is minor, the contract will be legally upheld and enforceable. A unilateral mistake will not make a contract unenforceable.

A unilateral mistake happens when only one party is mistaken about the terms or subject-matter.

Mistake as to the Identity of a Party

A contract can be void if there was a **mistake in the identity of a party**. The contract can be void if the plaintiff *can prove* that when the agreement was made, the plaintiff assumed the other party's identity was important. The other party is usually aware of the mistaken identity

Mistake as to the identity of a party can be divided into two categories:

1. **Where the contract is formed by post** (not face-to-face)

   The contract is void because the plaintiffs suppose they are contracting with a company they know and this is an important mistake as to identity.

2. **Where the contract is formed *inter praesentes*** (face-to-face)

   Here there is a strong belief that a party will contract with the party in his physical presence.

 Mistake as to the Possibility of Performance

The mistakes as to possibility of performance can be physical, legal and/or commercially impossible, although these mistakes are classified as common mistakes; the impossibility of them is rare. These types of mistakes are generally those which can not be performed within one year.

 Mistake as to the Subject Matter

A mistake as to the subject matter is the mistake made during the agreement where both parties are not aware of the mistake. In fairness, such a mistake will render a contract voidable. This most often occurs in circumstances involving the purchase of goods.

 Statute of Frauds

The Statute of Frauds (SOF) is an English law from 1677, adopted by the United States. The law necessitates that some contracts be documented in writing and that they be signed by all of the parties involved to make the contract enforceable and binding. The Statute of Frauds was created to help to prevent fraud or other injuries, such as perjury. The Statute of Frauds accomplishes this prevention by stipulating that certain contracts are not to be enforced or considered to be valid unless a documented agreement exists and if the parties have signed the agreement. Once it is signed, the parties are bound to accept the terms and the agreement will be enforceable and binding.

The English Statute of Frauds was enacted by Parliament in 1677 and only applied to particular kinds of contracts. It included promises to a creditor of another to pay that individual's debts, marriage contracts, sales of real estate, and a contract that cannot be carried out within one year of the formation of the contract. States have extended the statute to other types of contracts, such as life insurance contracts, for example. Except for New Mexico, Louisiana and Maryland, all states have recognized and have enacted the statute of frauds into law.

The six types of contracts that are under the Statute of Frauds and must be in written form are:

Marriage – Promises in consideration of marriage

Year – Contracts that by their terms *are impossible* to complete within one year

Land – contracts involving the sale of land

Executor – promise to pay an estate's debts from the executor's private funds

Goods – some contracts for the sale of goods

Suretyship – Contracts to answer for the debt of another

These types of contracts spell "MYLEGS" which is a memory trick to help you memorize them.

A party who sues for any type of fraud or for breach of contract in a "MYLEGS" related case must prove that a written contract is in existence, as the burden of proof lies with the defendant.

In the 1970's it was discovered that many US companies operating in foreign countries were paying large bribes (totaling over $300 million) to high government officials to ensure that preferential treatment and business was given to their companies. Of course, the United States was not alone in the practice of bribery. In countries around the world, bribery is a normal part of business and a common practice. However, in 1977 the Foreign Corrupt Practices Act was passed, making it illegal for any United States citizen to bribe a foreign official. It also made it illegal for anyone (citizen or not) on United States soil to further such payments.

Within the United States the policy is useful for decreasing corruption in business, but it can be a great disadvantage to international businesses because bribery is not illegal in other countries. Therefore, if an American business were to compete with a business from another country to contract on a job, the other country would be able to bribe officials to get the contract where the American business would not. This technically puts American firms at a disadvantage to all other firms in a global sense.

 Breach of Contract

When it comes to business, there are disputes all the time, especially over contracts. This is why it's always a good idea, whenever money or anything of value is an issue, to draw up a contract. When someone breaches that contract, it means that one party did not hold up their end of the bargain and is now trying to back out of a deal. When someone breaks or breaches a contract, it can be enforced and the injured party can try to recover any financial, physical, or mental harm caused by this breach of contract. To enforce a contract, many disputes are resolved through the court system. When the dispute is between $3000.00 to $7000.00 dollars, both parties settle in a small claims court.

A breach by *anticipatory repudiation* means that the party will not, can not or intends not to fulfill their responsibilities some time in the future. An anticipatory breach gives the non-breaching party the option to treat a breach as immediate, and to terminate the contract and sue for damages *before* the breach actually occurs.

A *partial breach* (immaterial breach or a minor breach) is the failure to meet a set term of the contract that is so small, it does not cause a complete breach of contract. A partial breach can be solved by a small adjustment.

A *repudiatory breach* (*fundamental breach*) of contract breach is a breach that is so fundamental that it allows the offended party the right to discontinue actions of the contract, along with the right to sue for damages.

A *material breach* is any failure to perform that allows the other party to the contract to either force action, or collect damages due to the breach of contract. A significant failure of the performance of a contract allows for a force of action or to permit the injured party to sue for damages.

There are **remedies to a breach of contract** that can be resolved out of court. The injured or wronged party in the contract is permitted to a "relief" under the law. There are many kinds of damages and the following are just a few examples.

When a person wins a lawsuit, they are often awarded some form of relief. Relief is basically a form of compensation for whatever it was that a person was in court over, being physical harm, damage or a violation of their rights. Relief comes in two different forms: damages and injunctions. An injunction is an order from a judge requiring that the losing party either do or refrain from doing something. For example, a restraining order, which requires that an individual refrain from going near another individual, is a type of injunction.

Damages are monetary compensation that the winner, or victim, in a lawsuit receives. Damages can be applied to nearly any type of case, including situations in which there is a breach of contract. **Damages** are most commonly used when a breach of contract happens. Payments in cash are usually awarded to the injured party of the breached contract. The following are the different types of damages that can be awarded to the offended parties.

Compensatory damages aim to put the non-beaching party in the position that they would have been in if the breach had not occurred.

Punitive damages are payments that the breaching party has to pay to compensate the non-breaching party. Punitive damages are meant to punish the offending party for their wrongful acts.

Liquidated damages are specific damages that were previously identified by the parties in the contract itself, in the event that the contract is breached. These damages are to be a reasonable estimate of actual damages that might result from a breach of contract. For example, a tenant in an apartment who doesn't pay their rent essentially costs the landlord the amount that they could have received if they had upheld their end of the contract.

Finally, **nominal damages** are awarded in situations where there is no (or very little) actual financial loss involved. They are also used in situations where the plaintiff cannot adequately prove the extent of an injury or loss. Typically, the amounts involved with nominal damages are small, such as one dollar, or just the amount of the lawsuit.

Specific Performances may be used as a remedy for breach of contract if the subject matter of the agreement is rare or unique, and damages would not suffice to place the non-breaching party in as good a position as they would have been had the breach not occurred.

Attorney fees and costs – can only be awarded if the contract specifically states they will be given.

Consequential and Incidental Damages – money for loss as a result of the breach that was predictable (*foreseeable damages*), meaning that both parties knew that, at the time of the contract, there would likely be a loss if a breach occurred.

Rescission – the contract is mutually canceled and both sides are exempt from performance and money advanced is refunded.

Reformation – the terms of the contract are altered to clearly present the original intentions of both parties.

# *Cancellation and Restitution*

The injured party may cancel the contract and sue for restitution, which then places the injured party back in the same position they were in before the breach. Cancellation of contract voids the contract altogether and relieves both parties from any obligations within the contract.

One important consideration for businesses to keep in mind is the age of their customers. Minors, or customers under the age of 18, are not considered to have the capacity to enter into a contract. Therefore, contracts entered into by a minor are void, or invalid. This does not refer only to written contracts, but also implied or oral ones – such as the assumed agreement to pay in the future. This means that a company has no legal precedence on which to demand payment or compensation for any goods or services that a minor consumes. This fact is true whether or not the company is aware of the person's age. If the minor is silent about their age or lies outright the company is still legally responsible for the goods, not the minor or their guardians.

Scope and Meaning of Contracts

The scope of the contract is the most significant part of the contract. The scope of the contract will clearly state what work will be performed, as well as what is not a condition of the contract and work that is not to be performed. In most circumstances, the exclusions outlined within the contract will have great importance to the scope of the contract.

The meaning to a contract is to have a formal document which contains the agreement of parties and which serves as evidence of the obligation. The contract will also include the general and supplementary terms and conditions as well as the administrative and technical requirements.

When parties form a contract, they most likely have set ideas to its terms and meaning. This idea, internal belief, of the contract's meaning is called *"subjective intent."* (It is your personal belief as to the 'meaning' of the contract.)

Assignment and Delegation

An assignment is a transfer of rights and a delegation is an appointment of another to perform one's duties. Contract rights can be assigned freely; however, where the assignment would vary materially the duty of the obligor, increase materially the burden of risk imposed by the contract, or impair materially the obligor's chance of obtaining a return performance, then the rights may not be assigned. The right to delegate one's contractual duties to another is limited by the rule that when a person contracts with another to do work or perform a service and the person employed has been selected with reference to his individual skill, a substitute performance by another party need not be accepted. Assignment transfers the interest of the assignor. The assignee stands in the shoes of the assignor, taking his rights and remedies subject to any defenses which the obligor has against the assignor prior to notice of assignment. One way to get around this rule, that the obligor may assert against the assignee any defense he could assert against the assignor, is to become a holder in due course. A holder in due course takes commercial paper free of any defenses that prior parties may have been able to assert.

DISCHARGE OF CONTRACTS

A contract can be discharged by performance, agreement, breach or frustration.

PERFORMANCE

The general rule is that parties must perform exactly all the terms of the contract in order to discharge their obligations. For example: if the contract is for the sale of six red apples, then there should be six red apples. The goods have to agree with the descriptions to the letter.

AGREEMENT

The rule here is what has been created by agreement may be extinguished by agreement. An agreement by the parties to an existing contract to extinguish the rights and obligations that have been created is itself a binding contract, provided that it is made under seal or supported by consideration. Where the agreement for discharge is not under seal, the legal position varies according to whether the discharge is bilateral or unilateral.

Bilateral discharge happens when both parties to the contract have some right to surrender, whether there has been a non-performance by either party, or only a partial performance by either party.

ACCORD AND SATISFACTION

Each party may want to cancel their present agreement and nothing more. When there is an agreement mutually to release the other from the obligations under the first agreement, there is an accord and satisfaction.

RESCISSION AND SUBSTITUTION

Each party may intend rescission of the original contract and substitution of a new contract.

VARIATION

Each party can agree on the difference of an existing contract.

WAIVER

When one person voluntarily agrees to a request by another to give up his right of claim.

UNILATERAL DISCHARGE

Only one party has the right to surrender. Where one party has entirely performed his part of the agreement, he is no longer under obligations but has rights to compel the performance of the agreement by the other party. Unless the agreement is under seal, a consideration must be furnished in order to make the agreement enforceable.

FRUSTRATION

Due to a change in circumstances, a contract is rendered impossible to perform, or it has become deprived of its commercial purpose by an event not due to the act or default of either party.

Some examples of frustration of contract are:

- The destruction of the specific object essential for performance of the contract
- Personal incapacity – either party in the contract becomes incapacitated
- The non-occurrence of a specified event may frustrate the contract
- Interference by the government may frustrate the contract
- Supervening illegality – if a contract later becomes illegal
- Delay – unexpected delays may frustrate a contract

Illegal Contracts

Illegal contracts are forbidden by the legislature and, of course, our court system. Even if one or both parties do not know the contract is illegal, it's still unenforceable and no one is under obligation to follow its rules. If a person is unaware of any question to a contract's legality, his or her performance may be said to be in **misreliance on the contract**. However, ignorance is not bliss in this instance because if one signs an illegal contract, his or her ignorance is immaterial in the law's eyes. If a person believes the contract is illegal, and signs it anyway, he is said to **assume the risk** of what may or may not happen with this contract.

Discharge of Contracts

The act of canceling a contract or agreement and causing it to be null is to discharge a contract. There are many ways in which a contract may be discharged. The two most common methods of discharging of a contract voluntarily are **accord and satisfaction**.

ACCORD:

The agreement to accept a performance supplementary to that which was agreed upon under a previous contract.

SATISFACTION:

The performance of the conditions of that accord. Both elements must take place for there to be discharge by these voluntary means.

NOVATION:

The replacement of one of the original parties with a new party by the agreement of the three parties. A new contract is formed with identical terms of the original contract; only one party has been discharged and replaced with a substitute party.

IMPOSSIBILITY OF PERFORMANCE:

Impossibility of performance focuses on two distinct and separate categories in regards to the discharge of a contract.

SUBJECTIVE IMPOSSIBILITY:

The lack of ability of the individual promisor to perform, for example by illness or death.

OBJECTIVE IMPOSSIBILITY:

Meaning no one can carry out the performance. The destruction of the subject matter of the contract or the frustration of its purpose are types of objective impossibility.

The discharge of a contractual duty may also come about through a merger or statutory release. A merger occurs when one contract is stopped because it is combined with another contract.

One difficulty that often arises when doing business with companies in different countries is the issue of enforcing a contract. Because countries all have their own legal systems, it can be difficult to come to a resolution with foreign companies when there is a breach of contract. Because it is often the case that foreign courts are less likely to be concerned with enforcing a contract, it is recommended that within any contracts it is specified that any disputes will be resolved in a United States court (typically a specific state, the one in which business is done, is named). From there, as long as all of the legal proceedings are legitimate and properly handled, most countries will accept any arbitration as binding for the foreign company as well. It is also helpful to have an adequate understanding of the legal system of the foreign company to ensure that disputes are resolved in a timely manner.

Agency

An **agency** is a lawful relationship where one person will act on behalf of another person (called the principal). The agent is authorized to make negotiations on behalf of the principal or create a contractual relationship between the principal and the third party. This branch of law separates and controls the relationships between the Agents and the Principals; the Agents and the Third Parties; and the Principals and the Third Parties.

Agency can be created by a written, implied, express or oral contract, or created by estoppel. An agency can also be formed in an emergency situation without express consent to do so. Agency laws will vary by state.

The Principal must give the Agent the authority to act on their behalf (except in certain situations where the agent will act in an emergency on behalf of the principal).

The two major types of authority include:

- **Actual authority**

    Actual authority occurs when the Principal's words or actions cause the Agent to trust that they have been allowed to act. This may be from a contract or implied. If it is apparent that the Principal gave actual authority to Agent, actions of the Agent will bind the Principal. This will be the outcome even if the Agent behaves dishonestly for his own advantage except if the Third Party knew of the Agent's own personal agenda. If there is not a contract but the Principal's words or behavior reasonably led the Third Party to think that the Agent was allowed to act then the Principal will be bound.

- **Apparent authority**

    If the Principal's words or behavior would lead a Third Party to believe that the Agent was authorized to act for the principal. If a Principal gives the impression that an Agent is authorized but there is no actual authority, the Third Parties will be protected if they have acted reasonably. This is often referred to as "Agency by Estoppel" and sometimes as "Doctrine of Holding Out."

Because the scope of responsibilities of the federal government is so large, often legislators will create what are called Administrative Agencies to carry out specific duties. An Administrative Agency can have characteristics of executive, judicial or legislative branches. There are literally hundreds of Administrative Agencies, and each one is unique in its scope and duties. Typically an agency will be under the jurisdiction of the executive branch, and be associated with a specific cabinet or department. For example, some Administrative Agencies include the Environmental Protection Agency (EPA), Federal Reserve Board (Fed), United States Postal Service (USPS), Federal Trade Commission (FTC), Securities and Exchange Commission (SEC) and many, many more.

As mentioned, the agencies may have characteristics of any of the branches of government. They may have the authority to create new regulations (similar to executive powers), mediate disputes (a judicial power), or to prosecute violators of laws (a legislative power). The main difference between the powers of Agencies and the government is that the agency creates regulations, whereas the government passes statues or laws. There are specific processes that an agency must follow in creating regulations.

Employment Contracts and Law

It's always a good idea to read the employment contract before you go to work for a company of any kind. The employee contract tells you the conditions of your employment, what your wages will be, how many hours they expect from you and the kind of work you will be doing for them. It also depends on what position you will have when you go to work for them. The conditions below should be within any employee contract your read:

- Terms of employment.
- Duties of the employee including general and specific responsibilities and performance of duties.
- Compensation including monthly salary, automobile expenses, relocation and moving expenses, and a one-time bonus inducement if used. Details such as bonus

or incentive plans, stock options, salary deferment plans, disability benefits, and health and retirement plans may or may not be spelled out.

- Confidentiality required of the employee regarding employer's operating expenses, pricing formulas, procedures, trade secrets, and proprietary information. This confidentiality extends to employee lists, customer lists, or prospective customers who become clients of the organization during the individual's term.
- A non-compete clause.
- Provisions for termination including a violation of responsibility, an inability to perform duties, reorganization, or low company profits. Higher-level employees frequently have a clause included in the contract to state a certain amount of money, often from six to twelve months' salary, that will be paid to the employee in the event of termination by disagreement or dispute.

Any item not covered in the original employment contract falls under common-law rights. This means that every employee owns the rights to all ideas, inventions, or discoveries unless he/she was specifically hired to develop those ideas or inventions. If the idea or invention is the incidental result of employment, then the rights belong to the employee unless otherwise specified within the employee contract.

Title VII

The final set of laws that regulate businesses are those which promote equality and safety. When it comes to equality, the primary law involved is Title VII of the Civil Rights Act of 1964. According to Title VII a person may not be discriminated against based on their race, color, religion, gender or nationality. The applications of the law are fairly straightforward, a business cannot refuse to hire someone, or do business with someone, on a basis of any of those factors. In cases where the business can prove that, for example, that the job can only be done by a specific gender then it is allowed (however, exceptions cannot be applied on a basis of race).

The Civil Rights Act also created the Equal Employment Opportunities Commission (EEOC). The EEOC was created to ensure that the Civil Rights Act was enforced, and conduct investigations in cases where there may be violations.

Affirmative Action

The EEOC also helps in the implementation of programs which promote equality involving the areas mentioned in the Civil Rights Act. These programs are called affirmative action programs. Affirmative action basically describes programs which seek to reduce or reverse the effects of discrimination, as opposed to merely "not practicing" it.

The term affirmative action was first used by President Kennedy in stating that federal money used be used to "take affirmative action" in ending discrimination. Shortly after, the Civil Rights Act was passed and signed by President Johnson. President Johnson described the idea behind affirmative action by comparing life to a race. He said that you cannot take a person who has been chained up for years and, putting them at the starting line of a race, believe it to have been fair. Although the term affirmative action can be used to apply to any form of discrimination (such as gender or age), most often people consider and use it in terms of discrimination based on race or color.

Affirmative action programs have been applied not only to workplace discrimination, but also to education as well. Many universities began practicing policies designed to increase the number of minority students attending the university. While there is support for such programs, affirmative action programs have also faced a wide amount of criticism.

In one famous case, **Regents of the University of California vs. Bakke**, Allan Bakke sued a medical school he had been applying to for rejecting his application multiple times. Allan Bakke was white and the school had set quotas dictating that at least 16 of the applicants admitted must be of minority races. Although Bakke could prove that his admittance criteria were better than the accepted minority applicants, the minority applicants were accepted so that the school could meet its quota. Bakke claimed that this was a violation of the Equal Protection Clause of the Fourteenth Amendment. The Supreme Court ruled in his favor 5-4, deciding that although the school could consider race as an acceptance criteria, the strict guideline of a specific numerical quota was not allowable. As time progresses, businesses and universities continue to look for ways of both implementing affirmative action programs and not creating "reverse discrimination" against the minority group.

Comparable Worth

Another equality issue which aims at correcting past injustices is comparable worth. Virtually all statistics show that even today the average female worker makes only about two thirds of what the average male worker does. The theory of comparable worth is that this is a result of widespread past discrimination against women. The idea is that jobs typically held by women receive lower pay on average than jobs typically held by men because those jobs were devalued in the past. Advocates of comparable worth work to ensure that jobs typically held by women that involve the same levels of work and risk as other jobs, receive the same level of pay.

Other examples of laws promoting equality ensure equal pay for men and women working the same jobs (Equal Pay Act), prohibit discrimination based on age (Age Discrimination in Employment Act) and prohibit discrimination based on pregnancy or related medical conditions (Pregnancy Discrimination Act).

ADA

There are also many other laws in addition to the Civil Rights Act which address issues of equality. For example, the Americans with Disabilities Act (ADA) which is designed to ensure that people with disabilities receive the same opportunities for work as people without disabilities. The act applies to all government agencies and labor unions. The law also extends to private employers with more than 15 employees. Within a workplace the law can be applied to practices such as hiring employees, firing employees and promoting employees. For example, under the ADA a business may be required to install a ramp leading to the front doors to ensure that employees confined to a wheelchair are equally able to work. This sort of practice is referred to as reasonable accommodation, and it is required under the law. Another example of reasonable accommodation could be purchasing a specialized machine that could be used by a blind employee. The law does not require that any sort of preferential treatment be given to disabled employees or applicants. An employee is free to choose to hire the most skilled employee and fire the least skilled employee based on the qualifications required for a job.

OSHA

Many laws also focus on protecting the safety of employees. For example, the Occupational Safety and Health Administration (OSHA) was created to ensure that business employ proper safety methods and maintain safe working conditions. It specifically protects workers against workplace hazards. For example, it dictates that moving parts must be covered so that a worker couldn't happen to contact it and injure themselves, sets limits on the amount of chemical that a worker can be exposed to, regulates the use of protective equipment for dangerous work environments and many other aspects of worker safety as well.

FLSA

The Fair Labor Standards Act (FLSA) is a federal law regarding employment guidelines. It establishes minimum wages, overtime pay rules, youth or child employment regulations, and other standards. The FLSA requires that employees are paid at least a certain established minimum wage (as of 2009 the minimum wage is $7.25 per hour), and that one and one-half times that rate be paid for time worked over 40 hours in any 7 day period. The law also requires employers to inform employees of the FLSA standards and to keep records of pay and time worked. Child labor also falls under the jurisdiction of the Fair Labor Standards Act. The requirements are aimed at ensuring that work does not interfere with school schedules, and that minors are given safe working conditions. The regulations are overseen by the United States Department of Labor.

Sales Contracts

A sales contract should set the terms, conditions and price of each sale. This insures that both the business and the buyer are covered, and it helps keep disputes about details like payment terms, late fees and penalties down to a minimum. The contract does not have to be anything fancy, or long, and as with most things, the rule is, keep it simple. The contract should include the details below.

- **Price:** It's one of the most important things in the contract; make sure the contract includes any price adjustment and discounts, as well as installation and delivery charges (if any).
- **Credit and payment terms:** If you give credit to your customers, be very specific about the payment terms and finance charges for any late payments.
- **Warranties:** These should be limited; however, there is no law stating you can't make it longer than the usual 90-day warranty. Warranties need to state that goods will be free from any defects and conform to specifications for a fixed amount of time.
- **Limited, liability claims:** Attempts to limit your liability and inform the buyer that the amount of liability is equal to the price of the item. Liability claims do not always stand up in court so they're not always enforceable. However, there is no harm in stating that you will not be held responsible for any damages, either punitive or speculative that may occur over the use of the product.
- **Disclaimers:** Make these stand out in bold print because you want to show that your company complies with certain provisions of the UCC, (Uniform Commercial Code). The UCC helps to simplify laws governing commercial transactions and keeps things uniform among various jurisdictions. Each state is different when it comes to commercial codes so make sure to look into your state's UCC codes.

 Torts

A tort is a civil wrong or a wrongful act towards another, that causes harm to that person, whether it's intentional or accidental. Torts cover all negligence cases as well as intentional wrongs which result in harm. Tort law is one of the biggest areas of law and results in more civil litigation than any other category of law. Many intentional torts can also be crimes, assault, battery, wrongful death, fraud, theft and trespass on property and form the basis for lawsuits for damages by the injured parties. Defamation of character, intentionally telling harmful lies about another person, either in print or broadcast—liable, or orally—slander, is also known as a tort. Tort law describes the obligations, the rights, and the remedies in civil cases to provide relief for any persons who have suffered harm or damage from the negligent acts of others. The person who sustains injury or suffers damages is called the plaintiff, and the person who is responsible for causing the injury or damage is called the defendant.

United States tort law differs from state to state. Jurisdictions permit actions for negligent causes of emotional distress even if there is no present physical injury to the plaintiff, but many jurisdictions do not permit this. For any type of tort, states vary on the causes of action, remedies, statutes of limitations, and the amount of evidence the parties can/must show

Three (3) elements must be present in **every** tort action.

- The plaintiff (injured party) must show that the defendant was under a legal obligation to act in a certain way.
- The plaintiff must establish that the defendant was negligent in their obligations or did not behave accordingly.
- The plaintiff must demonstrate that he/she suffered injury or obtained a loss or damage as a consequence of the defendant's violation or negligence.

The word *tort* is derived from the Latin word *torquere*, which means *wrong*.

Tort law serves four purposes:

- **Compensates victims** for injuries suffered by the negligent actions (or inaction) of others.
- **Shifts the cost** of injuries to the party (or parties) who are responsible for causing them.
- **Discourages** careless behavior in the future.
- **Supports** legal rights that have been neglected.

Everyone is responsible for his or her actions, not only for the result of their willful actions, but also for an injury that may happen to another by his/her ordinary care of skill in the management of his or her property or person. The definition of negligence is the doing of something which a reasonably prudent person would not normally do, or, the failure to do something which a reasonably prudent person would do, under the same circumstances. All in all, the failure to use ordinary or reasonable care.

A **tortfeasor** is a person who commits a tort. Tort law considers the rights and remedies available to persons injured through other people's carelessness or intentional misconduct. Tort law can also hold people responsible for other people's injuries regardless of who is to blame or if the injury was caused by negligence or not.

An **intentional tort** is when one person hurts another by willful, positive or aggressive conduct. It is when the tortfeasor intends a particular harm to result from his/her actions of misconduct. There are several types of intentional torts.

- Battery
- Assault
- False imprisonment
- Infliction of emotional distress
- Fraud
- Misrepresentation
- Malicious prosecution
- Abuse of process
- Defamation
- Trespass
- Conversion
- Slander of title
- Disparagement of goods
- Defamation by computer

Negligence is the failure to do something that a reasonable person would do in the same circumstances, or the doing of something a reasonable person would not do. Negligence is a wrong generally characterized by carelessness, inattentiveness or neglectfulness rather than by a positive intent to cause injury. What distinguishes negligence from an intentional tort is that negligence does not require the intent to commit a wrongful action, but the wrongful action is sufficient to constitute negligence. Misconduct negligence is when someone was hurt as the result of unreasonable carelessness.

Strict liability and absolute liability is the liability for an injury whether there was negligence or not. The most important type of strict liability is ***product liability***. This is when a manufacturer or seller of a dangerous or defective product is held liable for injuries or damages this product caused. People who are owners of wild and dangerous animals are also subject to absolute liability if someone gets hurt by these animals.

Other things that are found to be so dangerous they impose absolute liability are the use of chemical sprays and the storage of a large amount of natural gas in populated areas. Also included, the storage of explosives and blasting operations that result in property damage or personal injury. Absolute liability is different from intentional torts because the intent to commit an absolute liability tort does not matter. The tortfeasor is held responsible under absolute liability no matter how careful they were or how many precautions were taken.

Property Law

If you own a piece of land, it is said that one can lawfully rule over things, objects and land. Land, in general, includes the face of the earth and everything of permanent nature over or under it. This includes any structures, minerals, gems, oil, etc. There are many divisions when it comes to real property classification, but the most important are freehold estates, non-freehold estates and concurrent estates.

- Freehold estates are estates that a person has ownership for as long as he or she and their heirs want to own the property. Freehold means "fee simple absolute," another term for this would be "life estate," and this means the person retains possession of the property for as long as he or she lives.
- Non-freehold estates have a limited duration, this includes tenancy for years, tenancy at will and tenancy of sufferance.
- Concurrent estates exist when property is owned or possessed by two or more people simultaneously.

Most states have exclusive jurisdiction over the land within their borders. Real estate transactions are governed by a wide body of federal statutes and the state statutory and common law. Each state establishes different state law requirements. Real estate contracts require that the property being sold is done so by the marketable value at the time of the sale. The owner (seller) must show proof of ownership (title) and make sure that if there is a third party, he or she has no undisclosed interests in the title. Usually, during the sale of real estate a title insurance company or an attorney will be hired by a buyer in order to investigate the property to make sure everything is on the up and up. They will investigate the title and make sure no liens are held against it and make sure the property itself is marketable. Title insurance companies also insure the buyers against any losses or damages that may happen during any part of the transactions.

Probate is an interesting part of property law. When a person dies their possessions are transferred and divided among friends, family, charities or the government. How this is to be done is often stipulated in a will, but if no will is available it goes to the government to decide. This process of dividing a person's estate (possessions and assets) is referred to as probate. The area of law which handles matters of probate is referred to as probate law. The process begins when a probate court determines whether a will is valid. Then an executor is named and begins the process of carrying out the will. Any additional problems which arise, if heirs wish to challenge a will, petitions are filed, there are outstanding claims against the estate or any other number of difficulties, it falls under the category of probate law.

Personal Property

Personal property refers to property that can be moved from one place to another. *Movable property* is items that are *tangible*. These legal ideas were created from English Common Law. Except for land, personal property can be subject to possession. Personal property can be separated into two groups:

- **Corporeal personal property:** includes such property as animals, jewelry; etc. Property that is capable of touch and sight.

- **Incorporeal personal property:** includes property such as stocks and bonds. Also includes copyrights, trademarks and patents. This is the *existence* of tangible property. Intellectual property refers people's ideas or inventions. There is a set of laws referred to as intellectual property rights laws which govern and protect intellectual property. Different types of intellectual property are protected in different ways, with some examples being patents, copyrights and trademarks. Patents are used when a person invents something, and gives the holder a right to prevent others from manufacturing it. A patent can only be obtained for information or products which a person or business can prove is new and non-obvious. In other words, they must have actually invented something. A copyright covers materials that are written. A trademark refers to words or names that can be identified with specific companies and products. For example, logos, symbols and brand names are all types of trademarks.

Bailment refers to a situation in which an individual, the bailor, transfers some personal property to another individual, the bailee. For a transfer of personal property to be bailment it must be understood that the transfer is only temporary, and both parties have the intention of returning it in the future. While the goods are in the possession of the bailee they have responsibility for and control over them and their use. There are two different types of bailment: constructive bailment and gratuitous bailment.

Constructive bailment creates a legal obligation between the bailor and bailee. It is for the mutual benefit of both individuals. An example of constructive bailment could be a repair shop. In this situation the owner of a good transfers their bike to the possession of the repair shop, and they fix it for a fee. This is also the case with shipping companies.

Gratuitous bailment does not create an obligation of payment, but rather benefits either the bailor or the bailee. For example, if an individual has their neighbor care for their pets while they go on vacation, bailment has occurred which is beneficial only to the bailor. They temporarily transfer ownership of their pets, but without the obligation to compensate their neighbor. On the other hand, an example of bailment which benefits the bailee would be a library. The bailee would rent the book from the library, constituting a temporary ownership, but free of charge.

Product Liability

Product liability is a touchy subject among business owners but it's a very vital part of owning a business. You need to cover all aspects of your business, you, your employees, your products, etc. Product liability pertains to the legal liability of manufacturers and sellers to compensate buyers, users and even the people around you and your business. Everything needs to be protected from any damages or injuries suffered because of defects of any goods purchased. This is one place where Torts come into play because they make a manufacturer liable if his/her product is defective and becomes dangerous to the user. Ultimate responsibility for injury and damage cases will fall on the manufacturer to make good for any damages or harm, but liability can go farther than just to the manufacturer. It can also include the retailer, wholesaler or middleman and lessor. Bigger cases can also involve people outside of the manufacturing and distributing process like a certifier. The responsibility will more than likely be imposed by an action from a plaintiff against the manufacturer directly, or by a claim indemnification, which may come from a cross claim or a third party claim by the retailer or wholesaler or anybody else who might be held liable for the injury caused by a defective product. In modern principles of product liability, with the elimination of privity requirements, in most instances, recovery is no longer limited to the purchaser of the product or even a user but can also extend to a non-user, usually someone who was in the wrong place at the wrong time and became injured or damaged by a defective product.

Product liability laws manage the legal responsibility of manufacturers, distributors, and vendors for damages resulting from dangerous or malfunctioning products.

Product liability laws protect customers from dangerous products, while holding the manufacturer and retailer responsible for bringing to the marketplace goods or products that they should have known were dangerous or defective. Product liability often will involve retail goods, but can involve anything that can be sold.

Product liability cases can be brought under several theories, depending upon local law.

Manufacturing defects: liability that occurs from a defect caused from the manufacturing process.

Marketing defects: liability that occurs from a marketing error, involving issues such as insufficient warning labels or instructions.

Design defects: liability that occurs from an error in the design of a product, which makes it dangerous when used.

It may be feasible for a plaintiff to go after multiple liabilities.

Strict liability is when under a stringent liability standard, after the plaintiff proves that a product is faulty, legal responsibility results from that fact only regardless of how much care was used during design, manufacture and sale.

To prove **negligence** the plaintiff must usually show that the parties liable for bringing the product to the market had a responsibility to offer goods suitable for their expected use, and had they used reasonable care would not have failed to meet their responsibility, and that the plaintiff was wronged by the product as a result of the fault while using the product.

A warranty is an assurance from one individual or company to another that a certain terms or conditions will be met. Typically warranties are used in the context of an individual purchasing a product, and the seller guaranteeing a certain standard for that product. Warrantees come in a variety of forms. Some examples include express warranties and implied warranties. An express warranty is a formal, legal agreement. They are specific and will generally be written down. An example of an express warranty would be a retailer guaranteeing to replace any product which malfunctions within a year – essentially they are guaranteeing that the product will operate as desired for at least one year. An implied warranty, on the other hand, is not written down or formally stated. There are two basic types of implied warranties: warranty of merchantability and warranty of fitness for use. A warranty of merchantability is a statement of quality implied in the product itself. In other words, it is the expectation that the product is of the same general quality of other similar goods. A grocery store which sells melons that look nice on the outside, but are rotten on the inside, would be in violation of the warranty of merchantability. A warranty of fitness for use describes an understanding that the product will fulfill its intended use properly. If a company markets a car as being fit for off-road driving, but it is not actually designed for it, it would be a breach of warranty of fitness for use.

Breach of Warrant is when the plaintiff claims the breach of the written warranty connected with a product. Under a breach of *implied* warranty, the plaintiff claims that even though there is no direct warranty or the defect claimed is not protected by the direct warranty, a fault in the product causes it to be unsuitable for the intended purpose.

Employee Liability

In job situations where employees are required to engage in dangerous acts liability often becomes a matter of concern. Strict liability is a legal doctrine which allows a manufacturer or company to be held responsible for any damages, regardless of negligence or fault on the side of the user. This type of liability is generally applied to situations in which the action taken by the company was inherently dangerous. For example, transporting or using dynamite or other explosives is generally considered inherently dangerous. If a company is using explosives at a construction site and an individual wanders to close and is injured, it is likely that the company will be held responsible under strict liability. This is true whether or not the company took required precautions.

Liability also comes into question when the actions of employees are considered. In most cases the employer is liable for any acts of employees while they are doing company business. If an employee is inexcusably negligent, or even if there is simply an accident, the employer is responsible for any resulting damages. For example, an employee for a cable company is driving to fix a customer's cable connection and gets in a car crash. The company is responsible to pay any damages. On the other hand, if the same individual is in a crash while going to the grocery store one Sunday and they drive the company's car, the company is not responsible for the damages because the employee was not working at the time.

Insider Trading

Insider trading also has important ethical consideration in business. Insider trading describes when a company's insider (who are considered to be any official or owner who possesses ten percent or more of the company's stock) buy or sell stock. Insider trading can occur in ways that are legal or illegal. Legal insider trading occurs when a person legally trades stock within their own company. To prevent insiders from trading stock often, they are restricted from buying and selling stock within a six month period.

This way they make their stock decisions on a basis of how they believe that the company will perform long term. To trade legally, insiders must also report their trades to the SEC within two business days. Illegal insider trading occurs when an insider gains information about the company which is not available to the public and considers that information in buying stock. Insider trading can apply to not just the insider, but also their friends, family or employees who have access to nonpublic information. Any person who gives a tip to an outsider and shares nonpublic information that could influence their trading decisions could also be accused of insider trading.

Whistle Blowing

A whistleblower is a person who comes forward with information exposing wrongdoing by or within a company. Even in cases when it may seem like the employee is responsible to keep information about their employer's work private, such as if the corruption involves information in an NDA, the employee is legally obligated to expose the corruption. Whistle blowing can occur at many levels, involve many different forms of corruption and have many different eventual results.

For example, whistle blowing could occur on a small scale. If an employee were to discover that another employee was stealing paper, staplers, light bulbs or other sorts of office supplies from the company and then selling it online, then informing their supervisors would be a form of whistle blowing. On the other hand, whistle blowing can occur on a much larger scale, in which case the informant would have to possibly go to authorities to report the problem. For example, if the head accountant at a major firm was creating false contracts to increase the publicly reported net income, it would be the responsibility of anyone who discovered this to inform the manager or even government agencies which are responsible to prosecute those who are discovered committing accounting fraud.

One example of large scale whistle blowing would be the Enron scandal. The accounting fraud and misappropriation of money by the company's executives was exposed by an employee, Sherron Watkins, the Vice President of Corporate Development. Her actions resulted in investigation of the company which revealed the millions of dollars stolen from the company and the arrest of those responsible.

Both of the examples given refer to accounting fraud, but whistle blowing can relate to any activity which an employee believes to be either illegal or unethical. However, in order to protect the rights of the business and protect their privacy, it is important that a person consider whether the issue in question is truly unethical or illegal, and not just a matter of different interpretations of policy or ethical standards between management and employees that could be easily resolved. Examples of reasons for whistle blowing could include violations of health and safety regulations that are meant to protect workers or regulations which are designed to protect the environment, untruthful advertising slogans or campaigns, bribery, discrimination or theft.

There are also many different responses that can occur as a result of whistle blowing. Often those who discover corruption are afraid to come forward with their knowledge out of fear of the consequences that may befall them. In one famous case involving Kerr-McGee, a company which produced plutonium pellets to fuel nuclear reactors, an employee named Karen Silkwood noted that the security measures at the plant were not inadequate and not in line with regulations. She began building a case, but soon died under mysterious circumstances. However, that sort of situation is rare, and in some cases whistleblowers are even promoted to higher positions within a company because of their actions.

There are numerous laws and regulations which are designed to encourage and protect whistleblowers. For example, the Whistleblower Protection Act. This act protects employees of the federal government who expose incidences of waste of funds, abuse of authority, violations of laws or any other issue from any action being taken against them. If an employee feels that they are being retaliated against in some way, then they may file a complaint and have the issue taken care of.

Another protection developed for whistleblowers is the False Claims Act. The False Claims Act works from the opposite end of the Whistleblower Protection Act and encourages employees to expose efforts by companies to avoid paying federal taxes, providing false information to the federal government, conspiring to do either of those things or other acts which involve fraud towards the federal government. The act allows for compensation to the whistleblower of between 15 and 30 percent of the amount recovered as a result of their informing.

A third act with implications for whistleblowers is the Sarbanes-Oxley Act. The act has four elements relating to whistleblowers. The first is that a company must have a system of internal auditing through which an employee can file complaints. The second is that the act creates a legal responsibility for lawyers to inform on clients who are in violation of SEC regulations. The third is that the act prohibited any form of retaliation by employers to employees who legally inform about ethics violations to the proper sources, and provided the whistleblower with compensation for any legal fees. The fourth element of the act is that it allows for violators of any of the other elements can be charged under criminal law.

 Commercial Paper

Commercial papers are short-termed, unsecured debt papers issued by a business or corporation, usually used for financing of accounts receivable, inventories and meeting short-term liabilities. These are usually a discount security where the investor purchases a note at less than face value and receives the face value at maturity. The difference between the purchase price and the face value is called a discount. Sometimes commercial paper is issued as an interest-bearing note if the investor requests it. Commercial papers usually don't last over nine months and the debt is usually issued at a discount and reflects the interest rates of the times. Commercial papers are not backed by anyone nor have any form of collateral sustaining them so only firms with high-quality debt ratings will find buyers easily enough without having to offer a substantial discount for the debt issued. The main reason many financial businesses use commercial papers is because they don't need to be registered with the SEC Securities and Exchange Commission as long as each paper matures within the nine-month time limit. Because of this, commercial paper is a very cost effective way to offer financing to some business clients. Commercial papers are limited and can only be used on current assets and are not allowed to be used on fixed assets without SEC involvement. Commercial papers are issued by a wide variety of domestic and foreign businesses, and are favored by banks and finance companies. Finance companies provide people with car loans, home loans and unsecured personal loans and provide businesses with many short- and medium-term loans.

 Consumer Protection

Laws that protect consumers from unfair or deceptive practices are known as consumer protection laws. These laws have been created for almost every state, though the details of each state's law for consumer protection can differ. These state laws often permit a consumer to start a suit even if the abuse was unintended.

Two of the most common lawsuits involving consumer protection include Deceptive Advertising and Deceptive Pricing.

DECEPTIVE ADVERTISING

An advertisement is unlawful, under both federal and state law, if it is misleading or deceives consumers.

Consumers have the right to sue an advertiser under state consumer protection laws; for example, when buying a product while trusting a misleading ad. They have the option to begin a small claims lawsuit or join others in a lawsuit to sue for a larger amount.

DECEPTIVE PRICING

The two pricing practices most often presented in suits regarding misleading or deceptive prices are those that show false price comparisons to another business or presenting a product that is allegedly "free" when it actually has a cost.

PRICE REDUCTIONS

Presenting a decreased rate from the average price is a frequent sales technique. But the price is deceptive unless the previous price is the real price of the product.

PUNITIVE DAMAGES

In an average lawsuit, a plaintiff can sue only for her actual losses.

There are many state and federal laws to keep people safe from dishonest or fraudulent manufacturers and dealers when it comes to products and goods of all and any kind today. There are many kinds of fraud but one of the biggest ones today is auto fraud. Most adults by now have heard of the "Lemon Law." The Lemon Law is a state and federal law that helps people who find themselves in the nightmare of buying a brand new product, like a car, computer, boat, motorcycle, or RV, and discover that what they just paid a good bit of money for, does not work like it should, if at all. Because auto fraud is such a huge problem, and one of the reasons the Lemon Law came into existence in the first place, we're going to focus in on auto fraud. Not only does the Consumer Protection Agency help people with auto fraud but with everything involving the automobile business. Insurance companies, car dealers and manufacturers, extended warranty companies, service contract companies and the auto finance companies.

It is against the law in almost every state to sell a car that has been in an accident of any kind, and lie about it. This means that if you're buying a car from a dealer and you ask him if the car has been in an accident, and he tells you "no" when it has been, that's illegal. It's illegal to sell a car, new or used, that has been in an accident and has had damage, either structural, collision, or any other, without first telling this to the buyer. It's considered illegal to sell an unsafe vehicle or misrepresent a vehicle and lie in response to questions asked about the vehicle. If you ask a dealer if there's been any work done to the car you're about to buy and he tells you "no," that's illegal too.

Auto fraud can take place during any part of the purchasing process when buying a car, from the minute you walk into the showroom until you sign the contract; the following are a few things to look for when you're buying a car.

- Bait & Switch is when there's an ad for the sale of one car and when you get there, the dealer has something else to show you. Also, the ad is for one price, while the actual price is much higher than the one advertised.
- Improper inflation of the invoice price. This includes any add-ons or charges that are supposed to be included in the sale price.
- Salvaged and Flood-damaged vehicles. Failing to disclose that a car or truck has been "salvaged" after an accident or flood damage.
- New Dealer Returns are when a dealer tries to sell a "new car" to you when it's actually a car that someone else has brought back because of defects or mechanical problems.
- Odometer rollback is when a dealer rolls back the actual miles on a car.

When buying a car make sure you look over everything very carefully. Even if you're not an expert when it comes to cars, you can still tell when something doesn't look right to you. Look for any color changes in the paint and body work. When body work has been done, the paint will not match up exactly, no matter how well it's done. Check the odometer and make sure the numbers line up. Uneven numbers can be a sign of tampering. If you don't feel good about the car you're looking at and you feel you are not getting the right answers to your questions, move on. There's another car out there with your name on it, without the hassles of buying a "lemon" for a car.

UCC

The UCC is a code known in full as the Uniform Commercial Code. Essentially it is a code that governs the rules involved with commercial trade. Part of the reason for the UCC is to ensure that trading standards are relatively uniform across various states. Each state has the option to review the code, and then adopt it to the extent they desire. The UCC has been adopted in all states, although some states make minor adjustments to better meet the needs of their specific trading situations.

The UCC addresses matters such as bulk trades, contract provisions, credit rules, shipments, and commercial transactions. Because the UCC is a piece of United States legislation, it is not required in any other nations. For many years there were no uniform trading rules on an international scale, but in 2014 a UN conference in Vienna produced a treaty known as the CISG (Contracts for the International Sale of Goods) that has been ratified by most major countries. It was based on the principles of the UCC although it differs on several points.

The UCC has specific instructions regarding the delivery and acceptance of goods purchased under contract. Among these instructions is the fact that the goods must be in "perfect tender," meaning that what is delivered must be exactly what was contracted for. If goods are delivered that do not meet the qualifications of the contract, then they are referred to as nonconforming goods.

Goods could be considered nonconforming for any number of reasons. If the goods are broken, the wrong specification (color, size, shape), in the wrong quantity or if they are in any other way not in line with the terms of the contract then they are considered nonconforming. If a buyer determines upon inspecting the goods that they are nonconforming, they then have the option to either accept them, accept only some of the goods, or to reject the goods. If the goods are rejected then the buyer must give notice to the seller within a reasonable amount of time so that they may arrange to have the goods picked up.

EPA

The United States Environmental Protection Agency, or EPA, is the federal agency responsible for monitoring environmental matters in the country. They have the legal power to regulate and monitor environmental factors, and to administer fines and sanctions based on their results. Matters regulated by the EPA include water pollution, air pollution, pesticides, fuel, oil, drinking water, radiation, endangered species, and hazardous waste.

The EPA is headquartered in Washington DC, but has offices all across the country. The EPA has preventative, protective, and cleanup programs, and works with local and state governments to implement laws and programs approved by Congress. It is important that companies keep up-to-date with any legal requirements that may affect their operations so that they may comply with them.

CERCLA

The Comprehensive Environmental Response, Compensation, and Liability Act, also known as CERCLA or commonly as "Superfund," creates a method to manage hazardous waste sites that have been abandoned or are uncontrolled. It is commonly known as the Superfund because it imposes a tax on chemical companies in order to create a fund for cleaning up uncontrolled or abandoned hazardous waste sites for which the EPA is unable to find the liable company or individuals. This legislation authorized the EPA to take short term actions to address any release or potential release of chemicals requiring immediate actions, and also long term actions to clean up and eliminate hazardous sites that are on the National Priorities List of the EPA.

Endangered Species Act

The Endangered Species Act was passed in 1973 under President Richard Nixon. The act is designed to protect various designations of animal species. The act specifies three designations of monitored species: endangered, threatened, and candidate. Endangered species are the most threatened group. These are at a high risk of extinction and the agency seeks to rehabilitate them. Threatened species are similarly at risk, and are those species which are likely to become endangered in the near future if measures aren't taken. Candidate species are those which are being considered for status as either endangered or threatened. What is unique about the Endangered Species Act is that it protects not just the animals, but also the land and ecosystems in which they live. The act gives the Fish and Wildlife Service and the Oceanic and Atmospheric Administration the duty of overseeing the protections of these animals.

Clean Air Act

The Clean Air Act is a piece of federal legislation that was passed with the goal of monitoring and controlling air pollution. The act was first passed in 1970, but it has been amended several times as more information about air pollution has become available. The Clean Air Act requires that the Environmental Protection Agency (EPA) establish standards for monitoring and controlling air pollution. The act targets pollution produced by both stationary and non-stationary objects.

This means that it includes not only factories, but also vehicles, aircrafts, and other possible pollutants. The act requires that major sources of pollutants (which are defined as those capable of producing more than 10 tons of harmful pollutants in a year) set goals to reduce their emissions as much as possible. The EPA is responsible to regularly review these goals and pollution levels.

Clean Water Act

The Clean Water Act was passed shortly after the Clean Air Act and is a piece of federal legislation that targets the levels of water pollution. The original legislation, or Federal Water Pollution Control Act, was enacted in 1948 but with later amendments in 1972 it became known as the Clean Water Act. Similar to the Clean Air Act, the Clean Water Act gives the EPA authority to regulate the levels of water pollution by American companies. The law requires that any company who produces pollution must receive a permit from the EPA before allowing it to discharge into water sources. The EPA also monitors surface water quality and sets quality standards for wastewater and contaminants.

Terms to Know

Stare decisis: Latin, meaning *Let the decision stand*. This policy states the courts must adhere to time-honored decisions in previous cases.

Void: That which is insufficient for legal enforcement or not lawfully binding.

Valid: Legally binding and enforceable.

Voidable: That which is not exclusively void, but can be avoided.

Enforce: The act of reinforcing; to force obedience.

Unenforceable: Not capable of being enforced.

Enforceable: That which can be reinforced, or allows forced obedience.

Duress: A strong influence.

Counteroffer: An offer made by someone who has rejected a previous offer.

Buyer: A person that buys goods or contracts to buy goods.

Consumer: A person who buys goods or contracts to buy goods.

Delivery: The transfer of possession or control of goods.

Sale: Transfer of something (including ownership/title) in exchange for thing of value (money, services) under the terms agreed upon between the buyer and seller.

Fiduciary: A person who owes loyalty (and good faith) to another.

Assignee: The party who is assigned contract rights.

Assignment of rights: The transfer of the rights coming from a contract to a third party.

Assignor: The party who makes an assignment of their rights.

Delegation of duties: The act of assigning all or part of one's duty established in a contract to a third party.

Delegatee: The third party the delegator's duty is assigned to.

Delegator: The party who assigns his duty to a third party.

Obligee: The party who is owed a duty of performance.

Obligor: The party who owes another party a duty.

Forbearance: A promise not to do something.

Promissory estoppel: A non contractual promise that is still enforceable.

Quasi contract: A contract that is forced by the courts to prevent injustice.

Quo warranto: When a person's right to hold an office or governmental benefit is questioned.

Uniform Commercial Code: The law that governs contracts for sale of personal property.

Sample Test Questions

An important note about these test questions. Read before you begin. Our sample test questions are NOT designed to test your knowledge to assess if you are ready to take the test. While all questions WILL test your knowledge, some or all may cover new areas that are not previously covered in this study guide. This is intentional. For questions that you do not answer correctly, take the time to study the question and the answer to prepare yourself for the test.

1) Who invented the first known legal codes in 2000 B.C.?

   A) The Babylonians
   B) The Romans and Hebrews
   C) King Dungi of Sumer
   D) None of the above
   E) Both A & B

The correct answer is C:) King Dungi of Sumer.

2) What does lex talionis mean?

   A) We the people
   B) An eye for an eye
   C) Guilty
   D) Do no harm
   E) Both B & C

The correct answer is B:) An eye for an eye.

3) How long did the Dark Ages last?

   A) About 500 years
   B) About 1000 years
   C) About 10 years
   D) About 100 years
   E) The Dark Ages are a myth

The correct answer is A:) About 500 years.

4) What is the Mosaic Code?

   A) Gods special care and protection
   B) The foundation of Judeo-Christian moral teachings
   C) The basis of our U.S. legal system today
   D) All of the above
   E) None of the above

The correct answer is C:) The basis of our U.S. legal system today.

5) In 1066 England, what happened to help grow and standardize common law and justice throughout the land?

   A) The Norman Conquest
   B) The Ten Commandments
   C) Nothing major happened in 1066
   D) The Dark Ages were over
   E) The legal system was decentralized

The correct answer is A:) The Norman Conquest.

6) Where did the word "Sheriff" come from?

   A) It didn't come from anywhere, it just happened
   B) The leader of the 10 families called "tithings"
   C) The head of law enforcement of the Shire
   D) Both B & C
   E) The head of the 10 families

The correct answer is C:) The head of law enforcement of the Shire.

7) In which of the following cases would an offer not be valid?

   A) When one of the parties is not in agreement
   B) When one of the parties is a minor
   C) When the offer constitutes a social agreement
   D) When the offer not clearly defined
   E) All of the above

The correct answer is E:) All of the above. A valid offer constitutes a legal agreement between two parties of adequate mental capacity.

8) In medieval England, to prove a person was guilty, a red-hot piece of iron was laid in the accused hand. If the burn did not heal properly…

   A) The accused could go free
   B) The accused had to pay a fine
   C) The accused was considered guilty
   D) The accused was beheaded
   E) None of the above

The correct answer is C:) The accused was considered guilty.

9) Who was the first to use "traveling judges"?

   A) The Romans
   B) The Hebrews
   C) King Dungi
   D) King Henry II
   E) King Henry IV

The correct answer is D:) King Henry II.

10) Who was the sixth king of Babylon and wrote a famous set of written laws known as the Code of Hammurabi?

   A) King Hammurabi
   B) Moses
   C) King Henry II
   D) There are no "Codes of Hammurabi"
   E) Nobody really knows who the author really is

The correct answer is A:) King Hammurabi.

11) How does "common law" define murder?

   A) The killing of another human being by accident
   B) The unlawful killing of another human being
   C) The unlawful killing of another human being with malice
   D) Only criminal law defines murder
   E) Both B & C

The correct answer is E:) B & C. The unlawful killing of another human being and the unlawful killing of another human being with malice.

12) What is the definition of manslaughter?

   A) Death caused by passion
   B) Death caused by rage
   C) Death caused by negligence
   D) None of the above
   E) All of the above

The correct answer is E:) All of the above.

13) Before the American Revolution, American colonies were still under British law. When did the colonies start changing the laws to better suit their needs?

   A) After acquiring their independence
   B) After the Boston Tea Party
   C) The colonies were still under British rule until the 1800's
   D) Common law practices still guide modern legal codes
   E) None of the above

The correct answer is A:) After acquiring their independence.

14) In order for someone to be found guilty of murder, what two conditions have to be met?

   A) The planning of the crime/to carry the plan out
   B) To confide in another person of your plan/the intent to kill another
   C) The planning of a crime/the intent to kill with spite or hatred
   D) All of the above
   E) None of the above

The correct answer is D:) All of the above.

15) Which of the following is NOT used to protect intellectual property?

   A) Trademark
   B) Copyright
   C) Writ of certiorari
   D) Patent
   E) None of the above

The correct answer is C:) Writ of certiorari. Trademarks protect words or names identified with certain companies, copyrights protect written information and patents protect inventions.

16) A tort is….

   A) A civil action in which a person asks to be compensated for a personal harm
   B) A serious violation of the law
   C) The body of law that governs relations between individual persons
   D) Both A & B
   E) An editable piece of pastry

The correct answer is A:) A civil action in which a person asks to be compensated for a personal harm.

17) For a civil court to rule against a party, the proof against the accused must be_____.

   A) Beyond a suspect
   B) The preponderance of the evidence
   C) A reasonable doubt
   D) An unreasonable doubt
   E) Both A & B

The correct answer is B:) The preponderance of the evidence.

18) To be found not guilty of a criminal law, _____ is needed.

   A) Reasonable doubt
   B) Preponderance of the evidence
   C) Guilty by suspicion
   D) A jury of one's peers
   E) None of the above

The correct answer is A:) Reasonable doubt.

19) Which of the following would NOT be illegal under the Foreign Corrupt Practices Act?

   A) If an individual working for a Chinese company bribes a US Congressman to pass laws favorable to their company's operations.
   B) If a US company compensates a French official in return for giving them preferential treatment in business contracts.
   C) If a company pays a building inspector to overlook certain regulations when considering whether their offices are built in line with safety regulations.
   D) All of the above are illegal under the Foreign Corrupt Practices Act.
   E) None of the above

The correct answer is D:) All of the above are illegal under the Foreign Corrupt Practices Act. The Act makes it illegal for US citizens to further bribes, or for bribes to occur on US soil.

20) Criminal law is?

   A) Criminal law is a statement of written rules that people must conform to and defines which behaviors are allowable and which are not
   B) A statement of written rules that certain people must conform to
   C) A statement of written rules that criminal must abide by
   D) A statement of written rules that everybody must abide by
   E) Both B & C

The correct answer is A:) Criminal law is a statement of written rules that people must conform to and defines which behaviors are allowable and which are not.

21) Which of the following correctly identifies the qualifications to receive a patent?

   A) It must be non-obvious and new.
   B) It must be based on fact but non-obvious.
   C) It must be an improvement of an already existing product but unique.
   D) All of the above
   E) None of the above

The correct answer is A:) It must be non-obvious and new. In other words, they must have actually invented something.

22) What is the function of criminal law?

   A) Keeps criminals in check
   B) Functions help keep all people in line
   C) Help control social behaviors through its ability to punish and correct law violators
   D) Help us see who's bad and who's good
   E) None of the above

The correct answer is C:) Help control social behaviors through its ability to punish and correct law violators.

23) A fabric store has a strict policy of hiring only female workers. This is a violation of the

   A) ADA
   B) Civil Rights Act
   C) Equal Employment Committee
   D) Criminal Hiring Act
   E) None of the above, it is perfectly legal

The correct answer is B:) Civil Rights Act. The Civil Rights Act prevents discrimination on a basis of race, color, national origin, religion, and gender.

24) What is substantive criminal law?

   A) Law that defines what is legal and what is not legal
   B) Law that defines what kinds of punishment fits the crimes
   C) Law that defines what crimes are convicted by a jury or by a judge
   D) Law is the written code that defines crimes and their punishments
   E) All of the above

The correct answer is D:) Law is the written code that defines crimes and their punishments.

25) Mala Prohibitum means what?

   A) Crimes that reflect social values and public opinions
   B) Crimes that are illegal because of their violence
   C) Crimes that reflect a judge's opinion
   D) Crimes that are not violent
   E) Crimes that most people commit every day

The correct answer is A:) Crimes that reflect social values and public opinions. Mala Prohibitum are statutory crimes that violate laws that reflect social values and public opinion. Offenses like drug use, public drunkenness and prostitution are considered mala prohibitum.

26) An individual gets in an argument with their neighbor and throws a baseball at them. However, they have poor aim and the baseball hits a stranger walking by instead. The neighbor may sue for

   A) Battery
   B) Assault
   C) Assault and battery
   D) Neither assault nor battery
   E) None of the above

The correct answer is B:) Assault. Because they were intentionally threatening their neighbor with immediate violence, it qualifies as assault.

27) Why is a "meeting of the minds" not a good reason to form a contract?

   A) Because one doesn't know if the other person is of sound mind
   B) It is how contracts were formed in the early years of contracts and contracts often went bad
   C) Today this is not a good validation because it's hard to tell a person's true mind or intentions
   D) It's just as good today to form a valid contract as it was earlier
   E) Both B & D

The correct answer is C:) Today this is not a good validation because it's hard to tell a person's true mind or intentions.

28) Which of the following is NOT an example of an Administrative Agency?

   A) Securities and Exchange Commission
   B) United States Postal Service
   C) Department of Defense
   D) Federal Trade Commission
   E) None of the above

The correct answer is C:) Department of Defense. This is a department of the President's Cabinet, not an Administrative Agency.

29) In contract law, who actually creates a contract?

   A) The parties themselves to draw their own contract
   B) Created by a private party and then signed by the first party
   C) The lawyers to draw up a contract and then the party has to agree on it
   D) Only one person should write up a contract but others involved must agree before signing
   E) None of above

The correct answer is A:) The parties themselves to draw their own contract. Both parties work on their own contract together.

30) What is the lemon law?

   A) Promises that only one party has to agree to
   B) Promises that help consumers with their purchasing problems
   C) A law that may help consumers with their purchase problems
   D) A state and federal law that helps people find solutions when they have purchased a product that does not work
   E) The lemon law is the promise that the lemons people buy will be good and fresh

The correct answer is D:) A state and federal law that helps people find solutions when they have purchased a product that does not work.

31) A(n) _____ is an example of real property.

   A) Ebook
   B) Video game
   C) Article of clothing
   D) Piece of land
   E) None of the above

The correct answer is D:) Piece of land. Real property includes real estate or land and is immovable.

32) An individual agrees to lend their neighbor a car for the week when theirs breaks down. This is an example of

   A) Uncompensated bailment
   B) Bailor oriented bailment
   C) Constructive bailment
   D) Gratuitous bailment
   E) None of the above

The correct answer is D:) Gratuitous bailment. The bailment is gratuitous because only the bailee, in this case the neighbor, benefits.

33) For a contract to be legally binding, a promise must be exchanged for _____.

   A) Adequate consideration
   B) Sufficient consideration
   C) Any consideration
   D) Inadequate situation
   E) Inadequate consideration

The correct answer is B:) Sufficient consideration. Any previously agreed upon consideration that both parties agree to are required for a contract to be legally binding.

34) Which fraud has the broadest range of damages today?

   A) Computer fraud
   B) Auto fraud
   C) RV fraud
   D) Refrigerator fraud
   E) Any fraud is a big fraud

The correct answer is B:) Auto fraud.

35) How many elements are needed to form a contract?

   A) 4
   B) 5
   C) 6
   D) 3
   E) 8

The correct answer is C:) 6. Agreements, consideration, promise, legal capacity, consent, legality of objects, form are what are needed to form a contract.

36) The Supreme Court issues a(n) _____ to choose its cases.

   A) Injunction
   B) Writ of certiorari
   C) Federal Register
   D) Valid offer
   E) None of the above

The correct answer is B:) Writ of certiorari. A writ of certiorari is the process by which a higher court can review decisions and cases that took place in a lower court.

37) A consideration of a contract is_____

   A) The inducement, price or motive that causes a party to enter into an agreement or contract
   B) The inducement, sale or motive that causes a party to enter into an agreement or contract
   C) The inducement, motive or incentive that causes a party to enter into an agreement or contract
   D) The inducement, price or consideration that causes a party to enter into an agreement or contract
   E) None of the above

The correct answer is A:) The inducement, price or motive that causes a party to enter into an agreement or contract.

38) How did "consideration" come into law?

   A) Consideration were needed to form certain kinds of contracts
   B) A consideration is not always needed to form a contract, but it's good to have in most of them
   C) A person does not need a good reason for enforcing informal promises however an agreed upon exchange is always a good idea and makes everyone involved feel a bit better
   D) One needed a good reason for enforcing informal promises but an agreed upon exchange that would benefit the promisor also had to be included in order for the promise to happen
   E) Both C & D

The correct answer is D:) One needed a good reason for enforcing informal promises but an agreed upon exchange that would benefit the promisor also had to be included in order for the promise to happen.

39) What other types of auto fraud transactions does the Consumer Protection Agency help people deal with?

   A) Insurance companies, car dealers, extended warranty companies, service contract companies, etc.
   B) Insurance companies, car dealers, extended warranty companies, car wash dealers, etc.
   C) Insurance companies, car dealers, extended warranty companies, service personal, etc.
   D) Consumer protection agency only deals with auto purchases
   E) None of the above

The correct answer is A:) Insurance companies, car dealers, extended warranty companies, service contract companies, etc.

40) An obligation is considered a ____?

   A) Right
   B) Wrong
   C) Promise
   D) Duty
   E) Restriction

The correct answer is D:) Duty. All obligations are considered duties.

41) The branch of law which deals with matters of property or ownership is

   A) Possession law
   B) Property law
   C) Probate law
   D) Privatized law
   E) None of the above

The correct answer is B:) Property law. This can include real or personal property.

42) An individual takes their car to an auto shop to have the brakes refitted. This is an example of

   A) Uncompensated bailment
   B) Bailee oriented bailment
   C) Constructive bailment
   D) Gratuitous bailment
   E) None of the above

The correct answer is C:) Constructive bailment. It is for the mutual benefit of both individuals – the shop gets money and the individual gets a fixed car.

43) Why is it illegal to sell a bad car?

   A) Because it's wrong to lie
   B) It is considered illegal to sell an unsafe vehicle or misrepresent a vehicle and lie in response to questions asked about the vehicle
   C) Because it's wrong to sell a car that's been in a flood
   D) Because it's wrong to sell a brown car to a customer on Sunday's
   E) Because this transaction is not a part of the consumers protecting act

The correct answer is B:) It is considered illegal to sell an unsafe vehicle or misrepresent a vehicle and lie in response to questions asked about the vehicle.

44) Obligations are separated into which two distinctions?

   A) Imperfect obligations & perfect obligations
   B) Simple obligations & imperfect obligations
   C) Perfect obligations & agreeable obligations
   D) Short obligations & long obligations
   E) Whole obligations & perfect obligations

The correct answer is A:) Imperfect obligations & perfect obligations.

45) If you bought an RV and it ran great for the first but the next day it would not start and you continued to have mechanical problems, this would be called

   A) A tort law
   B) A criminal law
   C) A proper law
   D) A lemon law
   E) None of the above

The correct answer is D:) A lemon law.

46) Auto fraud can take place during any part of the car buying process, from the moment you walk into the showroom until

   A) You walk out again
   B) You ask if there's anything wrong with the car
   C) Before you sign the contract
   D) When you read the contract
   E) Until you sign the contract

The correct answer is E:) Until you sign the contract. Once the contract is signed, you have agreed to everything a dealer tells you.

47) Two classifications of non-legally binding contracts are, voids, and

   A) Torts
   B) Consideration
   C) Obligations
   D) Promises
   E) Voidable

The correct answer is E:) Voidable.

48) Express contracts are

   A) Contracts where implied agreement terms have been made at the time of the drawing of the contract
   B) Contracts where everyone is in a hurry so they all agree to the same thing at the time of drawing of the contract
   C) Contracts where terms are stated by the parties at the time of drawing up the contract
   D) Contracts where no one can agree at the time of the drawing of the contract so a later date has been set for another meeting
   E) Express contracts are non-existent

The correct answer is C:) Contracts where terms are stated by the parties at the time of drawing up the contract.

49) Implied contracts are

   A) Contracts whose terms are stated by the parties at the time of drawing up the contract.
   B) Contracts where there is an implied agreement although it's not in writing.
   C) Contracts are easily voidable because they are implied.
   D) Contracts that are drawn on a verbal agreement only.
   E) None of the above

The correct answer is B:) Contracts where there is an implied agreement although it's not in writing.

50) An agreement is

   A) The essential part of a contract
   B) Where at least one person has to agree to terms
   C) A word that must show up in a contract
   D) The union of two or more persons with a common goal in mind by expression of will words or conduct
   E) Both A & D

The correct answer is E:) Both A & D. The essential part of a contract, the union of two or more persons with a common goal in mind by expression of will, words, or conduct.

51) For a contract to be binding, consideration has to be legally sufficient. What does legally sufficient mean?

   A) The consideration has to be as good for the giver as it is for the receiver
   B) The consideration has to be without any strings attached
   C) The consideration must be legally detrimental to the person receiving or legally beneficial to the person making the promise
   D) The consideration must be legally acceptable to both parties
   E) A consideration must be legally voidable in the chance that either party wants out of the contract

The correct answer is C:) The consideration must be legally detrimental to the person receiving or legally beneficial to the person making the promise.

52) A preexisting duty is

   A) A promise to fix something that he or she broke
   B) A promise to do a job for a certain amount of money
   C) A promise to help another party serve their contract
   D) A promise to do what was supposed to be completed by another party
   E) None of the above

The correct answer is E:) None of the above. A promise to do what one person already has a legal duty to do; however, it does not constitute legally sufficient consideration because no legal detriment has happened.

53) How many sovereign form of government are in the U.S. today?

   A) 4
   B) 2
   C) 5
   D) 1
   E) 3

The correct answer is B:) 2. The government of the United States and the government of the many states.

54) What is federalism?

   A) The unlawful restraint by one person of the physical liberty of another
   B) The last action of a court where an appeal can be based
   C) A system of political organization with several different levels of government
   D) A formal accusation of a crime made by a proper public official such as a prosecuting attorney
   E) The determination to do a certain thing

The correct answer is C:) A system of political organization with several different levels of government.

55) Why did the founding fathers of our Constitution believe that our government needed to be divided?

A) Because our government would be too big if not divided
B) Because our founding fathers believe that "absolute power corrupted absolutely"
C) The founding fathers had nothing to do with forming our government
D) Because if our government was divided into too many parts, there would be no control of government
E) None of the above

The correct answer is B:) Because our founding fathers believe that "absolute power corrupted absolutely."

56) In which of the following cases is an employer NOT liable?

A) An employee misplaces a client's payment.
B) An employee crashes the company car while doing business.
C) An employee (with no criminal record) robs a grocery store over a holiday weekend.
D) All of the above
E) None of the above

The correct answer is C:) An employee (with no criminal record) robs a grocery store over a holiday weekend. Because it was not done as part of the employee's job, nor was it done on company time, the employer is not liable.

57) What is a jurisdiction?

A) The geographical area within which a court or public official has the right and power to operate
B) Studying a document and surrounding circumstances to decide the document's meaning
C) The background documents and records of hearings related to the enactment of a bill
D) Making a fake document or altering a real document with intent to commit a fraud
E) Both A & D

The correct answer is A:) The geographical area within which a court or public official has the right and power to operate.

58) Our U.S. Constitution is the 3rd highest form of law in the land and _____.

   A) Establishes a structure of our government
   B) Deals with all of our human rights
   C) Establishes a moral structure of our government
   D) Tells our government how they should run things
   E) Allows our government to do what they want

The correct answer is A:) Establishes a structure of our government. Our U.S. Constitution is the 3rd highest form of law in the land and establishes a structure of our government.

59) A document which creates a legal and binding agreement between two parties is a_____.

   A) Contract
   B) Allocution
   C) Jurisprudence
   D) Valid offer
   E) None of the above

The correct answer is A:) Contract. Contracts contain many elements, such as a valid offer and acceptance.

60) Which of the following has/is a responsibility to the safety and health of its citizens?

   A) The Supreme Court
   B) Final judgment order
   C) Police
   D) A presumption
   E) Model Penal Code

The correct answer is C:) Police.

61) _____ is the process of dividing a person's estate after their death.

   A) Federal Registration
   B) Injunction
   C) Jurisprudence
   D) Probate
   E) None of the above

The correct answer is D:) Probate.

62) What divides our government into three branches of power, executive, legislative and judicial?

   A) Principle of legality
   B) Police power
   C) False pretenses
   D) Separation of powers
   E) None of the above

The correct answer is D:) Separation of powers.

63) A construction company has an accident while working with dynamite and a number of individuals are injured as a result. The company is liable through

   A) Implied liability
   B) Contractual liability
   C) Strict liability
   D) Latent liability
   E) None of the above

The correct answer is C:) Strict liability. Strict liability is a legal doctrine which allows a manufacturer or company to be held responsible for any damages, regardless of negligence or fault on the side of the user.

64) How many court systems do we have in the U.S.?

   A) 6
   B) 8
   C) 3
   D) 5
   E) 2

The correct answer is E:) 2. There are trial courts and appellate courts.

65) What is a statute?

   A) The legal responsibility for damage or injury, even if you are not at fault
   B) Voluntary and active agreements
   C) To offer, give or receive anything of value in order to influence
   D) A law passed by a legislature
   E) Both B & C

The correct answer is D:) A law passed by a legislature.

66) Which of the following is NOT a requirement for a valid offer?

   A) The involved parties must be in agreement about the terms.
   B) The offer must constitute a legal obligation between the involved parties.
   C) The involved parties must have a preexisting agreement to collaborate.
   D) The terms of the agreement must be specific.
   E) None of the above

The correct answer is C:) The involved parties must have a preexisting agreement to collaborate. If there was a preexisting agreement there would really be no need for a new contract.

67) Why is it a good idea to have a contract when conducting business?

   A) Because if a dispute comes up, you want to be proven right
   B) When it comes to business, there are disputes all the time, and a contract keeps everybody honest
   C) Contracts are really not needed with today's business deals
   D) You want to make sure everybody is telling the truth, that's why it's good to get it in writing
   E) Contracts are a throwback from colonial days

The correct answer is B:) When it comes to business, there are disputes all the time, and a contract keeps everybody honest.

68) A waiver is

   A) When one person voluntarily agrees to a request by another to give up his right of a claim
   B) When both parties pull out of a contract
   C) When both parties waive their rights within the contract
   D) When one party asks the other to do more than what is within the contract and the other party agrees
   E) Both A & B

The correct answer is A:) When one person voluntarily agrees to a request by another to give up his right of a claim.

69) A _____ is an order that the case be returned to the lower court and that some action be taken by the judge when the case is returned.

   A) Records on appeal
   B) Statute
   C) Strict liability
   D) Provocation
   E) None of the above.

The correct answer is E:) None of the above. The correct answer is remand.

70) Which of the following is NOT an element of a contract?

   A) Valid offer
   B) Federal Register
   C) Acceptance
   D) Exchange of something of value
   E) None of the above

The correct answer is B:) Federal Register. The Federal Register is like the government's daily journal and contains information about operations.

71) What is civil law's primary purpose?

   A) Civil law's primary purpose is to compensate those who are injured by the fault of another
   B) Civil law's primary purpose is to compensate the manufacturer who was wronged due to frivolous lawsuits
   C) Civil law's primary purpose is to compensate a wronged homeowner
   D) Civil law's primary purpose is to punish manufacturers for making defective products
   E) Civil law has no primary purpose

The correct answer is A:) Civil law's primary purpose is to compensate those who are injured by the fault of another.

72) Which of the following does NOT describe the situations for which strict liability applies?

    A) If the situation is inherently dangerous
    B) There were not adequate precautions taken by the company
    C) An injury resulted when the user did not properly use the product
    D) Both B and C
    E) None of the above

The correct answer is D:) Both B and C. Strict liability applies regardless of precautions of the company or possible fault of the user.

73) _____ damages are meant to deter an individual from committing a crime again in the future and _____ damages are described in a contract as the result of a breach of contract.

    A) Punitive, liquidated
    B) Liquidated, compensatory
    C) Punitive, nominal
    D) Nominal, compensatory
    E) None of the above

The correct answer is A:) Punitive, liquidated. There are many different types of damages and the question describes punitive and liquidated damages respectively.

74) Which of the following is a person who owes loyalty (and good faith) to another?

    A) Assignor
    B) Fiduciary
    C) Obligee
    D) Obligor
    E) Consumer

The correct answer is B:) Fiduciary.

75) Congress is given power to

   A) To establish a post office and post roads, to punish piracy and other crimes of the high seas, to regulate interstate and foreign commerce, to declare war and raise armies
   B) To promote the arts, establish a post office, to declare war, to allow police to arrest offenders
   C) To regulate interstate and foreign commerce, to punish drug offenders, to punish counterfeiters, to establish a post office
   D) To coin money, to declare war, to promote the arts, to allow capital punishment
   E) To punish counterfeiters, coin money and fix standards of weights and measures

The correct answer is E:) To punish counterfeiters, coin money and fix standards of weights and measures. These are the fiscal and monetary powers of congress.

76) The area of law which handles the execution of an individual's will after their death is referred to as

   A) Probate law
   B) Property law
   C) Post-Will law
   D) Estate law
   E) None of the above

The correct answer is A:) Probate law. In other words, probate law refers to legal matters which relate to probate.

77) Two of the largest categories of civil law are

   A) Contract law and tort law
   B) Contract law and civil law
   C) Civil law and contract law
   D) Tort law and criminal law
   E) Both A & D

The correct answer is A:) Contract law and tort law.

78) Negligent, intentional and strict liability law are three types of _____?

   A) Criminal law
   B) Tort law
   C) Legal impossibility
   D) Legislative history
   E) Both C & D

The correct answer is B:) Tort law.

79) What is the main purpose of criminal law?

   A) To protect those who don't commit crimes
   B) To punish those who commit crimes
   C) People need a guide telling them the difference between right and wrong
   D) A guide to help the police to determine who breaks the law and who doesn't
   E) Both A & B

The correct answer is E:) Both A & B. The main purpose of criminal law is to prevent behavior that our society has determined to be undesirable. Its second purpose is to punish those who break those undesirable behaviors.

80) Which of the following is an example of an implied contract?

   A) A company signs an agreement with an individual to provide them with services.
   B) A person signs a loan to purchase a car.
   C) A person takes their car to a repair shop to get it fixed.
   D) All of the above
   E) None of the above

The correct answer is C:) A person takes their car to a repair shop to get it fixed. The implied contract is that once the car is fixed the person will pay.

81) What is the main purpose of civil law?

   A) To compensate those who committed a crime
   B) To punish those who committed a crime
   C) To compensate one for turning in another
   D) To punish one for selling drugs
   E) Civil law's primary purpose is to compensate those who are injured by the fault of another.

The correct answer is E:) Civil law's primary purpose is to compensate those who are injured by the fault of another.

82) Which of the following types of damages are specifically referenced within a contract?

   A) Punitive
   B) Liquidated
   C) Nominal
   D) Compensatory
   E) None of the above

The correct answer is B:) Liquidated. The purpose of liquidated damages is to cover any loss that would occur as a direct result of a breach of contract.

83) Oral slander is known as

   A) A criminal act
   B) A negligent act
   C) Defamation of character
   D) An unintentional wrong
   E) A fraudulent sale

The correct answer is C:) Defamation of character.

84) An example of a negligent tort is/are

   A) Accidents and medical malpractice
   B) A person wronged by someone else
   C) A person looking to sue a manufacturer for damages
   D) A person who robs a bank
   E) A person who beats up another

The correct answer is A:) Accidents and medical malpractice.

85) What is a tort?

   A) Behavior that causes a person to fear the infliction of immediate injury
   B) Offensive or harmful contact between two persons
   C) A civil wrong or wrongful act towards another person
   D) Behaviors recognized by the courts that require someone to take action, refrain from taking an action
   E) Defamation of character

The correct answer is C:) A civil wrong or wrongful act towards another person.

86) Do torts cover all negligent cases?

   A) No, they cover civil cases only
   B) No, they cover criminal cases only
   C) Yes, they cover both civil and criminal cases
   D) No, the only cover personal injury cases
   E) Yes, torts cover all negligent cases

The correct answer is E:) Yes, torts cover all negligent cases.

87) What actions are people held responsible for?

   A) The actions of their children and any children in their care
   B) Their own willful actions, but not if they didn't mean to cause an accident, or injure another
   C) Their own actions, whether intentional or not
   D) Their own actions, but not if a person doesn't know any better
   E) The actions of any of their family members in their presence

The correct answer is C:) Their own actions, whether intentional or not. All people are held responsible for their own actions.

88) Negligence is

   A) Failing to do something a person was supposed to do
   B) Doing something a person knows they shouldn't do
   C) Doing something that someone else was supposed to do
   D) Doing something that a reasonably responsible person would not normally do, or not doing something a responsible person would do
   E) None of the above

The correct answer is E:) None of the above. Negligence is when a person hurts another but not intentionally.

89) Three types of torts are

   A) Product liability, strict liability, and negligence
   B) Negligence, foreseeable liability and strict liability
   C) Product liability, foreseeable liability and intentional tort
   D) Strict liability, intentional tort and negligence
   E) Tort law, intentional tort, product liability

The correct answer is D:) Strict liability, intentional torts and negligence.

90) An intentional tort is when

   A) One person injures another but didn't mean to hurt anybody
   B) One person hurts another willfully
   C) One person say's something bad about another
   D) One person falsely imprisons another
   E) Both B & D

The correct answer is E:) Both B & D. One person hurts another willfully and one person falsely imprisons another. Both are intentional torts.

91) A tortfeasor is a

   A) Person who commits a tort
   B) Person who steals another's car
   C) Person who drinks too much
   D) Person who falls asleep with no warning
   E) None of the above

The correct answer is A:) Person who commits a tort.

92) A restaurant fires a waitress after learning that she has AIDS. Which law, if any, is this a violation of?

   A) Civil Rights Act
   B) Employee Privacy Act
   C) Americans with Disabilities Act
   D) Harrison Act
   E) None of the above

The correct answer is C:) Americans with Disabilities Act. The ADA extends protection against discrimination to individuals with disabilities, which includes diseases such as HIV or AIDS.

93) Four examples of an intentional tort are

    A) Battery, assault, fraud, misrepresentation, defamation
    B) Battery, assault, fraud, defamation, negligence
    C) Battery, assault, robbery, negligence
    D) Battery, assault, fraud, robbery
    E) Battery, fraud, defamation, negligence

The correct answer is A:) Battery, assault, fraud, misrepresentation, defamation.

94) A(n) _____ is awarded to the winner of a lawsuit in compensation.

    A) Damage
    B) Injunction
    C) Reward
    D) Relief
    E) None of the above

The correct answer is D:) Relief. Reliefs come in two forms: damages and injunctions.

95) A person orders new tires which are advertised as being for use in heavy snow, but when the tires arrive they are not suitable for winter use. This is a breach of

    A) Express warranty
    B) Warranty of merchantability
    C) Warranty of fitness for use
    D) Implied warranty
    E) None of the above

The correct answer is C:) Warranty of fitness for use. A warranty of fitness for use describes an understanding that the product will fulfill its intended use properly, which the tires don't.

96) What is product liability?

   A) The most important type of strict liability
   B) A manufacturer or seller of a dangerous or defective product is held liable for injuries or damages the product caused
   C) A manufacturer or seller of a product that helped a person and made their lives better
   D) A manufacturer or seller whose product broke before it was used
   E) None of the above

The correct answer is B:) A manufacturer or seller of a dangerous or defective product is held liable for injuries or damages the product caused.

97) What characterizes negligence?

   A) Attentiveness, caring, watchful and helpful
   B) The intent to hurt another
   C) Carelessness, inattentiveness, neglectfulness
   D) Carelessness, attentiveness, helpful
   E) Negligence, carelessness, inattentiveness

The correct answer is C:) Carelessness, inattentiveness, neglectfulness. These are the characteristics of negligence.

98) A U.S. company contracts with a foreign company to sell them products; however, the company breaks the contract and refuses to pay once they have been delivered. Which of the following statements is true?

   A) The U.S. company absolutely must sue for damages in the foreign country.
   B) As long as the legal proceedings are legitimate, the foreign company is bound by U.S. arbitration.
   C) There is no way for the U.S. company to get the money.
   D) The U.S. company broke the agreement so the contract is void.
   E) None of the above

The correct answer is B:) As long as the legal proceedings are legitimate the foreign company is bound by U.S. arbitration. It is recommended that within any contracts it is specified that any disputes will be resolved in a United States court (typically a specific state, the one in which business is done, is named), and other countries will recognize it as binding.

99) The difference between negligence tort and an intentional tort is

   A) There is no difference; they both mean the same thing
   B) Negligence requires the intent to commit a wrongful act
   C) Intentional torts have to be planned first
   D) Intentional torts don't really need the intent
   E) None of the above

The correct answer is E:) None of the above. Negligence is when someone hurts another unintentionally, and intentional is when a person hurts another and means to hurt them.

100) Misconduct negligence is?

   A) A person was hurt as the result of unreasonable carelessness
   B) A person was careful, but someone still was injured
   C) A person was hurt because someone's wild animal attacked him
   D) A person was hurt by name calling
   E) Nobody gets hurt

The correct answer is A:) A person was hurt as the result of unreasonable carelessness. This is misconduct negligence.

101) A car salesman gives the purchaser of a car a written guarantee that the brakes will last for at least 10 years. This is an example of a(n)

   A) Warranty of merchantability
   B) Implied warranty
   C) Warranty of fitness for use
   D) Express warranty
   E) None of the above

The correct answer is D:) Express warranty. An express warranty is a formal, legal agreement. They are specific and will generally be written down.

102) People with wild animals are held responsible for the actions of their actions, what kind of tort is this?

   A) Negligence
   B) Product liability
   C) Absolute liability
   D) Tortfeasor
   E) Misconduct

The correct answer is C:) Absolute liability. This makes people with wild animals responsible for their actions too.

103) What is product liability?

   A) A legal way for people to sue manufacturers for selling a defective product
   B) A legal way for a manufacturer to evade a consumer who wants to sue their company for damages
   C) The legal way for manufacturers and sellers to compensate those who may have been harmed by products made by them
   D) The legal way for manufacturers and sellers to disprove those who allege that the product made by them caused damages to their persons or property
   E) Product liability is the most important of all liabilities

The correct answer is C:) The legal way for manufacturers and sellers to compensate those who may have been harmed by products made by them.

104) Why do we have torts?

   A) Torts hold manufacturers and sellers liable for dangerous or defective products
   B) Torts make it possible for someone hurt by a damaged or defective product to claim compensation for the pain that was caused by a damaged or defective product
   C) Torts do not hold manufacturers and sellers liable as long as the damages or hurts caused were not that bad
   D) Torts allow people to hold the person responsible for making a defective or damaged product
   E) Both A & B

The correct answer is E:) Both A & B. Torts hold manufacturers and sellers liable for dangerous or defective products. Torts make it possible for someone hurt by a damaged or defective product to claim compensation for the pain that was caused by a damaged or defective product.

105) A person is walking down the street and gets run into by a person on a bike. As a result, they have a broken arm. If they sue the person on the bike for the money to cover doctor's bills, it would be referred to as

   A) Liquidated damages
   B) Nominal damages
   C) Compensatory damages
   D) Punitive damages
   E) None of the above

The correct answer is C:) Compensatory damages. Compensatory damages are awarded in an attempt to compensate the plaintiff for any loss, injury or harm that they may have come to.

106) Big liability cases can even go as far as the_____.

   A) Judge
   B) Lawyer
   C) Manufacturer
   D) Certifier
   E) None of the above

The correct answer is D:) Certifier. Some cases can be big enough they go all the way to the certifier.

107) An individual gets in an argument with their neighbor and throws a baseball at them. However, they have poor aim and the baseball hits a stranger walking by instead. The stranger may sue for

   A) Battery
   B) Assault
   C) Assault and battery
   D) Neither assault nor battery
   E) None of the above

The correct answer is D:) Neither assault nor battery. Because the injury was not intentional it qualifies as neither assault nor battery.

108) A commercial paper is?

   A) A deed
   B) A mortgage note
   C) A short-term unsecured debt paper that good for only 120 days
   D) A short-term unsecured debt paper
   E) A long-term unsecured debt paper

The correct answer is D:) A short-term unsecured debt paper.

109) Which of the following makes it illegal for US citizens to participate in bribes?

   A) Sarbanes-Oxley Act
   B) Anti-Bribery Act
   C) Foreign Corrupt Practices Act
   D) Whistleblower Act
   E) None of the above

The correct answer is C:) Foreign Corrupt Practices Act. The Foreign Corrupt Practice Act also makes it illegal for a person of any nationality to further a bribe while on United States soil.

110) What is the difference between the purchase price and the face value of a commercial paper called?

   A) A discount
   B) A disclosure
   C) A receipt
   D) A draft
   E) A value

The correct answer is A:) A discount. A discount is the difference between the purchase price and the face value of a commercial paper.

111) How long do commercial papers usually last?

   A) Two months
   B) Six months
   C) 10 months
   D) 90 days
   E) Nine months

The correct answer is E:) Nine months or 270 days.

112) Commercial papers are very cost effective ways to offer financing to clients, why?

A) Because they must be paid in full within 270 days
B) They don't need to be registered with the SEC Securities and Exchange Commission as long as it matures within the nine month time limit
C) Because they don't need to be backed or secured by anybody
D) They don't need any form of collateral to sustain them
E) None of the above

The correct answer is B:) They don't need to be registered with the SEC Securities and Exchange Commission as long as it matures within the nine month time limit.

113) What four things are needed before a Discharge of Contracts can occur?

A) Breach, performance, adjustment, frustrations
B) Performance, agreement, breach, consideration
C) Consideration, performance, agreement, breach
D) Performance, agreement, breach, frustration
E) Performance, agreements, frustration, adjustment

The correct answer is D:) Performance, agreement, breach, frustration.

114) What is an agreement?

A) An act of law where two or more persons declare their consent as to any act or thing be done, or not be done
B) An act of law between two people to get something done, or to help someone else
C) Two or more people agree to loan a third party a certain amount of money
D) An agreement between two or more people to impose a public duty
E) None of the above

The correct answer is A:) An act of law where two or more persons declare their consent as to any act or thing be done, or not be done. Two or more persons must give their consent they are both in agreement with the conditions.

115) Which of the following statements about administrative agencies is FALSE?

　A) They may have powers similar to any of the three branches of government.
　B) They typically operate under the jurisdiction of the executive branch.
　C) They are created by legislators to fulfill a specific purpose.
　D) They have to authority to create laws and statutes.
　E) None of the above

The correct answer is D:) They have the authority to create laws and statutes. Administrative agencies do not have the power to create laws; they create regulations or rules instead.

116) Performance is

　A) An act that someone does flawlessly
　B) A request that a judge makes during a trial
　C) Parties must perform exactly what's stated within a contract
　D) The failure to exercise a reasonable amount of care
　E) Parties can change their mind and void the contract

The correct answer is C:) Parties must perform exactly what's stated within a contract. A true performance means that all conditions within the contract as written.

117) What happens in a bilateral discharge?

　A) When a contract gets discharged because neither party can come to an agreement
　B) When one party in the contract surrenders
　C) One party fails to do what was agreed upon in the contract
　D) Both parties in the contract have the right to surrender
　E) Both A & D

The correct answer is D:) Both parities in the contract have the right to surrender.

118) An assignment and delegation is…

   A) An assignment is a transfer of rights and a delegation is an appointment of another to perform one's duties
   B) An assignment is when the court decides who is to do something within the contract and a delegation is the job of the other party
   C) There is no such thing as an assignment and delegation within a contract
   D) The assignment instructs one party to delegation the rules of the contract to another
   E) Voluntary and active agreements between both parties

The correct answer is A:) An assignment is a transfer of rights and a delegation is an appointment of another to perform one's duties. There has to be a transfer of rights and to appoint someone to perform the duties.

119) Why are there punitive damages?

   A) To make sure there are damages
   B) To make one party pay for damages
   C) An offer from one party to pay for damages to another
   D) To punish the offending party for their wrongful acts
   E) Punitive damages hurt everyone and nobody wins

The correct answer is D:) To punish the offending party for their wrongful acts. Punitive damages compensates people who are hurt or injured by someone else's mistakes.

120) What's a basic definition of Statute of Frauds?

   A) Requires that certain contracts be in writing, and that they be signed by all parties to be bound by the contract
   B) Requires that all contracts be written so a fraud cannot be committed
   C) Statute of Frauds is an old law and does not belong in our laws today
   D) An intentional fraud made by one party towards the other
   E) None of the above

The correct answer is A:) Requires that certain contracts be in writing, and that they be signed by all parties to be bound by the contract. The basic definition of Statute of Frauds requires that certain contracts be in writing, and that they be signed by all parties to be bound by the contract.

121) Under the Uniform Commercial Code, what is needed to satisfy a statute?

    A) The promise of one party to the other
    B) The writing to be done by one party and not the other
    C) A writing promising the sale of certain goods
    D) A writing promising not to sell certain goods on certain days
    E) The writing for the sale of goods need only be signed by the party to be charged, and a quantity term

The correct answer is E:) The writing for the sale of goods need only be signed by the party to be charged, and a quantity term. What the sale of goods is for and how many or how much.

122) What are joint obligations?

    A) No matter how many are involved in the contract, each person is only responsible for their own part
    B) Contracts that have only two people involved
    C) Contracts that involve four or more people
    D) This is a trick question and there is no such thing
    E) Contracts where only one person is responsible for making sure the contract is carried out by all

The correct answer is A:) No matter how many are involved in the contract, each person is only responsible for their own part. There could be over a hundred people involved in a contract, however, each person is only responsible for their part.

123) Which list of details makes a business contract?

    A) Warranties, claims, disclaimers, duress, price, limited liability clams
    B) Price, credit, warranties, limited liability claims, disclaimers
    C) Price, limited liability claims, disclaimers, warranties
    D) Warranties, price, credit, duress, disclaimers, limited liability claims
    E) Price, warranties, price, claims, disclaimers

The correct answer is B:) Price, credit, warranties, limited liability claims, disclaimers.

124) What is an employment contract?

   A) The contract that tells you how much you're getting paid, how long you're going to work and the kind of car you need to drive
   B) A contract tells you the conditions of your employment, what your wages will be, how many hours they expect from you and the kind of work you will be doing for them
   C) The contract that says how much you're not getting paid, the conditions of your employment, how many hours you're expected to work
   D) A contract that tells you the conditions of your employment, how many people work there, what time lunch is how much vacation pay you'll be receiving
   E) Both A & B

The correct answer is B:) A contract tells you the conditions of your employment, what your wages will be, how many hours they expect from you and the kind of work you will be doing for them. Depending on where you work your employment contract tells you how much, how many hours, and the kind of work you're expected to do.

125) A civil obligation is

   A) Obligations are not enforceable by law
   B) Obligations that pertain to only one party within the contract
   C) Obligations that if not carried out by one party must be done by another
   D) Obligations that can be taken to court and enforced by a judge
   E) Obligations that are binding an operation in law and give the other person the right to take things to court

The correct answer is E:) Obligations that are binding an operation in law and give the other person the right to take things to court.

126) Can a conditional obligation be suspended?

    A) No, conditional obligations cannot be suspended once signed
    B) Yes, conditional obligations can be suspended as long as both parties agree
    C) Yes, conditional obligations can be suspended if the condition has not been accomplished or the deal fall through
    D) Yes, conditional obligations can be suspended as long as everything within the contract are accomplished
    E) No, conditional obligations cannot be suspended because the law doesn't allow it once a contract is signed

The correct answer is C:) Yes, conditional obligations can be suspended if the condition has not been accomplished or the deal fall through. Conditional obligations can be suspended if the condition has not been accomplished or the deal falls through.

127) A 16 year old enters a bar and consumes a number of expensive drinks, assuring the bartender that they are 22. They later refuse to pay the bill. Which of the following statements is true?

    A) They are held liable for the goods they consumed because they lied about their age.
    B) The bartender may hold their parent's liable for the goods they consumed because they are underage.
    C) The bartender has no way to legally force either the 16 year old or their parent's to pay the bill.
    D) They should not have been allowed to consume the goods so they are only liable for half.
    E) None of the above

The correct answer is C:) The bartender has no way to legally force either the 16 year old or their parent's to pay the bill. Contracts entered into by a minor are void, or invalid.

128) A company hires an individual who is confined to a wheelchair; however, their offices are not wheelchair accessible. The ADA requires that the company

  A) Renovate their building only if it is convenient and fits the budget. Otherwise they can fire the individual once they realize their mistake.
  B) Renovate their building to be at least accessible to the individual – even if it requires a complicated process for them to complete tasks.
  C) Renovate their building to be universally accessible and the individual can complete tasks in the same manner as all other employees.
  D) Offer to let the employee work from home.
  E) None of the above

The correct answer is B:) Renovate their building to be at least accessible to the individual – even if it requires a complicated process for them to complete tasks. The ADA does not currently require universal design, just that it is accessible.

129) A large company decides that they are going to begin issuing stock, but do not register their stock with the Securities Exchange Commission. They are in violation of which law?

  A) Stock Registration Act
  B) Public Company Oversight Act
  C) Securities Exchange Commission Act
  D) Securities Act
  E) None of the above

The correct answer is D:) Securities Act. The Securities Act of 1933 created the SEC to ensure that companies were not fraudulently reporting and to create transparency in financial statements.

130) Which of the following is NOT under the jurisdiction of the FTC?

  A) Enforcing consumer protection laws
  B) Prevent and regulate monopolies
  C) Prevent fraud in securities reporting
  D) Investigate securities purchases
  E) None of the above

The correct answer is C:) Prevent fraud in securities reporting. This is the responsibility of the SEC.

131) The publication which includes the daily actions of various government agencies is called the

   A) National Journal
   B) Federal Register
   C) National News
   D) Federal Catalog
   E) None of the above

The correct answer is B:) Federal Register. The Federal Register is a type of journal for the government. It is published every business day and includes things such as the text of new laws, executive proposals and orders, and Federal Agency regulations.

132) If a person is denied the right to access the information on them in their credit report, this is a violation of the

   A) Administrative Procedural Act
   B) Truth in Lending Act
   C) Federal Register Act
   D) Fair Credit Reporting Act
   E) None of the above

The correct answer is D:) Fair Credit Reporting Act. This requires that individuals have access to the information about them, can submit information for updates, can dispute incorrect information, are aware of who has accessed their information and many other protections.

133) A textbook which discusses in depth the many aspects of law, included analysis and critique of different decisions could be considered a type of

   A) Jurisprudence
   B) Federal Register
   C) Fiduciary
   D) Valid offer
   E) None of the above

The correct answer is A:) Jurisprudence. The term jurisprudence may also be used to refer to specific types or branches of law, or describe anything which discusses law, compares it to other fields, or answers legal questions.

134) A(n) _____ is when a private company first offers stock to the public.

   A) Publicization
   B) Initial Public Offering
   C) Securities Option
   D) Stock launch
   E) None of the above

The correct answer is B:) Initial Public Offering. Before an Initial Public Offering (IPO), a company must register with the Securities Exchange Commission (SEC).

135) The EPA is a government agency and is therefore governed in establishing laws and procedures by which of the following?

   A) Fair Reporting Act
   B) Corrupt Practices Act
   C) Administrative Procedure Act
   D) Agency Regulations Act
   E) None of the above

The correct answer is C:) Administrative Procedure Act. This was created to regulate the ways in which government agency establish and enforce laws.

136) The manager of a public corporation is responsible for managing the corporation's assets on behalf of stockholders. This makes them a

   A) Fiduciary
   B) Administrator
   C) Federal register
   D) CEO
   E) None of the above

The correct answer is A:) Fiduciary. A fiduciary is an individual who has the responsibility for managing and caring for another's assets.

137) A judge rules that an individual who committed a crime must pay $2,000 to the victim of the crime. This is an example of which type of restitution?

A) Restitution fine
B) Parole revocation fine
C) Direct order
D) Victimization fine
E) None of the above

The correct answer is C:) Direct order. A direct order is a fine that must be paid to the victim. There are no limits to the amount of a direct order.

138) A company finds itself unable to make the payments on a loan they received. They meet with the bank to negotiate a new payment schedule, which they keep to until the loan is completely paid. This is an example of

A) Accord and Satisfaction
B) Compromise and Settlement
C) Agreement and Reconciliation
D) Accord and Settlement
E) None of the above

The correct answer is A:) Accord and Satisfaction. The parties met and renegotiated a contract and the new contract was successfully fulfilled.

139) Which of the following is NOT a benefit of a statute of frauds?

A) Reduces the chances of future litigation
B) Reassures contract signers that the contract is binding
C) Protects individuals from being cheated
D) All of the above are benefits of a statute of frauds
E) None of the above

The correct answer is D:) All of the above are benefits of a statute of frauds. A statute of frauds requires certain contracts to be in writing and signed by all involved parties.

140) When a person sues their neighbor for breaking a window in their house, they are operating under

   A) Criminal law
   B) Tort law
   C) Pecuniary law
   D) Compensation law
   E) None of the above

The correct answer is B:) Tort law. A tort deals with civil situations in which two individuals are battling each other. With criminal law the government is prosecuting and individual for violating a statute.

141) In which of the following situations would an employer NOT be in violation of Title VII of the Civil Rights Act of 1964?

   A) An employer of a small business with 20 employees refuses to hire any individuals that aren't white.
   B) The owner of a large factory purposely passes over females for promotions, and favors male workers.
   C) An employer refuses to hire a highly qualified individual for a position because they are gay.
   D) All of the above are illegal under Title VII.
   E) None of the above

The correct answer is C:) An employer refuses to hire a highly qualified individual for a position because they are gay. Title VII currently does not prohibit discrimination based on sexual orientation.

142) What is a breach of contract?

   A) Breach of contract is when one party doesn't sign the contract
   B) Its one of the many names of a contract
   C) Both parties agree on the same thing
   D) When someone breaches that contract, it means that one party did not hold up their end of the bargain and is now trying to back out of a deal
   E) None of the above

The correct answer is D:) When someone breaches that contract, it means that one party did not hold up their end of the bargain and is now trying to back out of a deal. All parties must complete all conditions of a contract, if not, there's a breach of contract.

143) When disputes over a contract are only $3000 to $7000 can the dispute be taken to court?

   A) Yes, a Small Claims Court
   B) No, things must be settled between parties
   C) Yes, but only the lawyers can attend
   D) No, the amount of damages is too small
   E) Yes, the Supreme Court

The correct answer is A:) Yes, a Small Claims Court. Any disputes between $1500 and $7000 can be taken to small claims court.

144) What are secondary obligations?

   A) Secondary obligations are not really obligations and will not stand up in court
   B) Secondary obligations make both parties hold to their promises
   C) Secondary obligations will back up primitive obligations
   D) Secondary obligations are the last to be done within the contract
   E) Secondary obligations are not real, no such thing

The correct answer is C:) Secondary obligations will back up primitive obligations. These are promises that if one condition has not been met, then at least a backup is there to get the obligation done.

145) What does termination of an offer mean?

   A) The end of the contract, all deals were met
   B) The contract is null and void
   C) The first offer was not accepted, a second one has to be made
   D) One party terminates the offer of the other
   E) None of the above

The correct answer is E:) None of the above. Both parties pull an offer and terminate the deal.

146) A bilateral mistake is when

   A) Both parties make a mistake
   B) One party makes a mistake
   C) Both parties believe they are getting the same thing
   D) One party receives one thing while the other party pays for it
   E) Both parties believe they are getting one thing when they're actually getting something else

The correct answer is E:) Both parties believe they are getting one thing when they're actually getting something else.

147) What does personal incapacity mean when it deals with contracts?

   A) Either party becomes ill or dies
   B) One party incapacitates the other
   C) One party does not like the other
   D) Both parties agree to disagree
   E) None of the above

The correct answer is A:) Either party becomes ill or dies. One or both parties are unable to continue a contract.

148) Which act created a Superfund for the cleanup of abandoned hazardous waste sites?

   A) Clean Water Act
   B) Clean Air Act
   C) CERCLA
   D) FLSA
   E) Environmental Monetary Fund

The correct answer is C:) CERCLA. CERCLA, or the Comprehensive Environmental Response, Compensation, and Liability Act, is commonly known as the Superfund because it imposes a tax on chemical companies in order to create a fund for cleaning up uncontrolled or abandoned hazardous waste sites for which the EPA is unable to find the liable company or individuals.

149) Which federal law sets minimum wage requirements?

   A) Clean Air Act
   B) Fair Labor Standards Act
   C) Minimum Allowed Act
   D) CERCLA
   E) None of the above

The correct answer is B:) Fair Labor Standards Act. This act sets requirements for minimum wage, overtime pay, recordkeeping, and child labor.

150) An employer believes that any company policy that increases overall profits is good. This follows which ethical philosophy?

   A) Virtue ethics
   B) Justice ethics
   C) Motivism
   D) Deontology
   E) Consequentialism

The correct answer is E:) Consequentialism. In this example, the employer focuses on the consequences of an action – in this case increased profits – to determine whether it is good or bad.

151) In which of the following scenarios would the contract be legally binding?

   A) A minor purchases a car from a dealership
   B) A minor signs a release that allows them to go skydiving even though they are under the legal age
   C) A minor purchases a game console from a store
   D) A minor purchases food from a grocery store
   E) None of the above

The correct answer is D:) A minor purchases food from a grocery store. Although in most cases a minor has the right to revoke a contract without a stated reason, when the contract was made to obtain the necessities of life it cannot be revoked.

152) The UCC is the

   A) Unanimous Commercial Code
   B) Uniform Contract Code
   C) Universal Commercial Code
   D) Uniform Commercial Code
   E) Universal Contract Code

The correct answer is D:) Uniform Commercial Code. The UCC is essentially a code that governs commercial trade in the United States to ensure that trading standards are uniform throughout the country.

153) A company orders 2000 blue pipes to build their product, but when the shipment arrives there are only 1900 blue pipes. This is an example of

   A) Nonconforming goods
   B) Partial acceptability
   C) Derived nonconformance
   D) Contract compatibility
   E) None of the above

The correct answer is A:) Nonconforming goods. Nonconforming goods are any goods that do not exactly match the terms of the contract. This can be a as result of quantity, quality, or other aspects.

154) The Clean Water Act gives which agency the power to regulate water pollution in the United States?

   A) Fish and Wildlife Services Agency
   B) National Oceanic and Atmospheric Administration
   C) Pollution Control Administration
   D) Environmental Protection Agency
   E) None of the above

The correct answer is D:) Environmental Protection Agency. The law requires that any company who produces pollution must receive a permit from the EPA before allowing it to discharge into water sources. The EPA also monitors surface qualities of waters and sets quality standards for wastewater and contaminants.

155) Which of the following would NOT fall under the jurisdiction of the EPA?

A) Air pollution
B) Endangered species
C) Interstate trade
D) Water pollution
E) Hazardous waste

The correct answer is C:) Interstate trade. The EPA, or Environmental Protection Agency, has the authority to oversee matters of environmental health throughout the country. This includes water pollution, air pollution, pesticides, fuel, oil, drinking water, radiation, endangered species, and hazardous waste among other things.

156) Which of the following is NOT a designation made by the Endangered Species Act?

A) Endangered
B) Candidate
C) Threatened
D) Vulnerable
E) All of the above are designations made by the Endangered Species Act

The correct answer is D:) Vulnerable. Endangered species are the most threatened group. These are at a high risk of extinction and the agency seeks to rehabilitate them. Threatened species are similarly at risk, and are those species which are likely to become endangered in the near future if measures aren't taken. Candidate species are those which are being considered for status as either endangered or threatened.

157) The case of Bakke vs. University of California called which matter into question?

A) CERCLA
B) Respondeat Superior
C) Fair Labor Standards Act
D) Clean Air Act
E) Equal Protection Clause

The correct answer is E:) Equal Protection Clause. Bakke argued that the 16 seats that were reserved for minority applicants violated his right to equal protection. The Supreme Court ruled that strict, specific quotas by universities did indeed violate this standard and ordered that Bakke be admitted to the university.

Introductory Business Law

158) Which of the following principles allows recovery on a promise even if there was no consideration or formal contract created?

A) Punitive remedy
B) Res ipsa loquitur
C) Respondeat superior
D) Promissory estoppel
E) None of the above

The correct answer is D:) Promissory estoppel. This is a legal doctrine which can be invoked if the promisee reasonably relied on the promisor to their own detriment. The courts will order performance by the promisor, assuming the promise was reasonable.

159) Samantha is arrested for fraud and her bail is set by the Judge, Martha, at $5,000. Samantha's friend Jonathan pays the money on her behalf to the jail employee, David. Who is the bailor in this situation?

A) Samantha
B) Martha
C) Jonathan
D) David
E) None of the above

The correct answer is C:) Jonathan. A bailor is a person who temporarily gives possession of a good to another to complete a bailment, as Jonathan did in this situation. When Samantha's case goes to trial, Jonathan will receive his money back. The bailee would be David because he is the one who has temporary care over the money.

160) An employee is negligent in managing the accounts of an important client. As a result, the client loses all of their money. The client then sues their employer. This is possible because of

A) Respondeat superior
B) Promissory estoppel
C) Restitution
D) Puffery
E) Quasi in rem jurisdiction

The correct answer is A:) Respondeat superior. This is a legal doctrine which means that the superior can be held accountable for the actions of employees. This is particularly true in cases where they should have been aware of those actions through proper supervision.

161) Which act requires major sources of pollutants to set goals that will reduce their emissions as much as possible?

   A) Clean Water Act
   B) Clean Air Act
   C) FLSA
   D) CERCLA
   E) Emissions Limitation Act

The correct answer is B:) Clean Air Act. The act requires that major sources of pollutants (which are defined as those capable of producing more than 10 tons of harmful pollutants in a year) set goals to reduce their emissions as much as possible. The EPA is responsible to regularly review these goals and pollution levels.

162) Which of the following is considered an equitable remedy?

   A) Nominal damages
   B) Specific performance
   C) Punitive damages
   D) Restitution
   E) All of the above

The correct answer is B:) Specific performance. Legal remedies come in the form of monetary compensation. When this is not sufficient to remedy the situation, a judge may elect an equitable remedy to the contract. For example, specific performance is an equitable remedy. This requires that the offending party perform the contract as written.

163) If a lawyer wishes to have the case moved to the city in which the majority of the witnesses live then he is using the principle of

   A) Promissory estoppel
   B) Respondeat superior
   C) Bailee
   D) Remedy
   E) Venue

The correct answer is E:) Venue. Venue refers to the location where the case is tried. Typically this will be where the original incident occurred or where the contract was executed. However, for matters of convenience either party may request a change in venue.

164) Which of the following is a legal advertising strategy?

A) Defamation
B) Puffery
C) Duress
D) Slander
E) None of the above

The correct answer is B:) Puffery. Puffery essentially means exaggeration, and is routinely used in promotion and advertising. These statements are mean to be viewed subjectively rather than literally.

 Test-Taking Strategies

Here are some test-taking strategies that are specific to this test and to other CLEP tests in general:
- Keep your eyes on the time. Pay attention to how much time you have left.
- Read the entire question and read all the answers. Many questions are not as hard to answer as they may seem. Sometimes, a difficult sounding question really only is asking you how to read an accompanying chart. Chart and graph questions are on most CLEP tests and should be an easy free point.
- If you don't know the answer immediately, the new computer-based testing lets you mark questions and come back to them later if you have time.
- Read the wording carefully. Some words can give you hints to the right answer. There are no exceptions to an answer when there are words in the question such as always, all or none. If one of the answer choices includes most or some of the right answers, but not all, then that is not the correct answer. Here is an example:

The primary colors include all of the following:

A) Red, Yellow, Blue, Green
B) Red, Green, Yellow
C) Red, Orange, Yellow
D) Red, Yellow, Blue
E) None of the above

Although item A includes all the right answers, it also includes an incorrect answer, making it incorrect. If you didn't read it carefully, were in a hurry, or didn't know the material well, you might fall for this.

- Make a guess on a question that you do not know the answer to. There is no penalty for an incorrect answer. Eliminate the answer choices that you know are incorrect. For example, this will let your guess be a 1 in 3 chance instead.

What Your Score Means

Based on your score, you may, or may not, qualify for credit at your specific institution. At the University of Phoenix, a score of 50 is passing for full credit. At Utah Valley State College, the score is unpublished. The school will accept credit on a case-by-case basis. Another school, Brigham Young University (BYU), does not accept CLEP credit. To find out what score you need for credit, you need to get that information from your school's website or academic advisor.

You can score between 20 and 80 on any CLEP test. Some exams include percentile ranks. Each correct answer is worth one point. You lose no points for unanswered or incorrect questions. On this particular test, you must answer 100 questions in 90 minutes.

Test Preparation

How much you need to study depends on your knowledge of a subject area. If you are interested in literature, took it in school, or enjoy reading then your study and preparation for the literature or humanities test will not need to be as intensive as that of someone who is new to literature.

This book is much different than the regular CLEP study guides. This book actually teaches you the information that you need to know to pass the test. If you are particularly interested in an area, or feel that you want more information, do a quick search online. We've tried not to include too much depth in areas that are not as essential on the test. Everything in this book will be on the test. It is important to understand all major theories and concepts listed in the table of contents. It is also important to know any bolded words.

Don't worry if you do not understand or know a lot about the area. With minimal study, you can complete and pass the test.

One of the fallacies of other test books is test questions. People assume that the content of the questions are similar to what will be on the test. That is not the case. They are only there to test your "test taking skills" so for those who know to read a question carefully, there is not much added value from taking a "fake" test.

To prepare for the test, make a series of goals. Allot a certain amount of time to review the information you have already studied and to learn additional material. Take notes as you study; it will help you learn the material.

Legal Note

All rights reserved. This Study Guide, Book and Flashcards are protected under US Copyright Law. No part of this book or study guide or flashcards may be reproduced, distributed or stored in a retrieval system, or transmitted in any form or by any means, electronic, mechanical, photocopying, recording, or otherwise, without the prior written permission of the publisher Breely Crush Publishing LLC. This manual is not supported by or affiliated with the College Board, creators of the CLEP test. CLEP is a registered trademark of the College Entrance Examination Board, which does not endorse this book.

FLASHCARDS

This section contains flashcards for you to use to further your understanding of the material and test yourself on important concepts, names or dates. Read the term or question then flip the page over to check the answer on the back. Keep in mind that this information may not be covered in the text of the study guide. Take your time to study the flashcards, you will need to know and understand these concepts to pass the test.

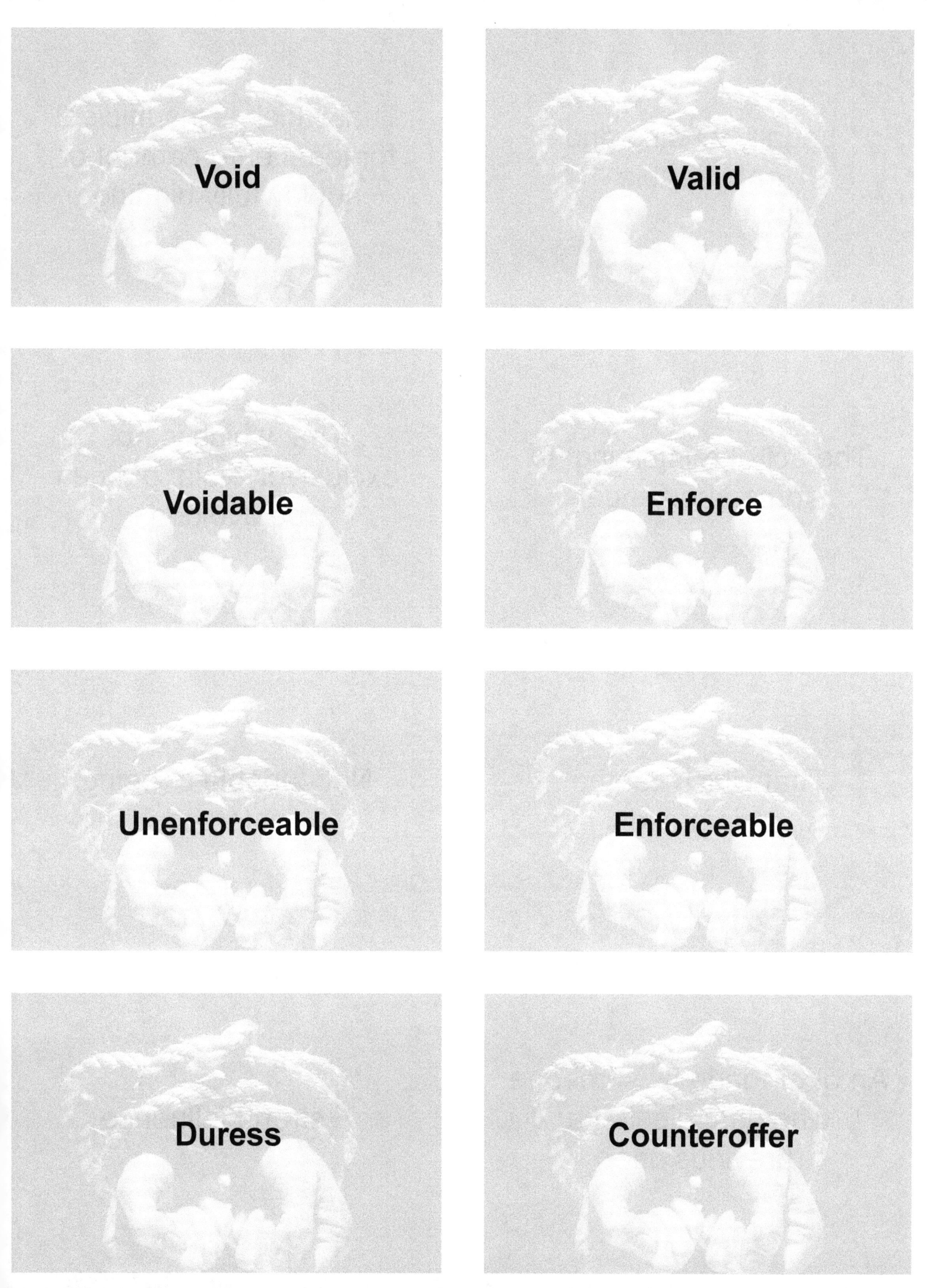

Legally binding and enforceable	That which is insufficient for legal enforcement or not lawfully binding
The act of reinforcing; to force obedience	That which is not exclusively void, but can be avoided
That which can be reinforced	Not capable of being enforced
An offer made by someone who has rejected a previous offer	A strong influence

Buyer	Consumer
Delivery	Fiduciary
Assignee	Assignment of rights
Assignor	Delegation of duties

A person who buys goods or contracts to buy goods	A person that buys goods or contracts to buy goods
A person who owes loyalty (and good faith) to another	The transfer of possession or control of goods
The transfer of the rights coming from a contract to a third party	The party who is assigned contract rights
The act of assigning all or part of one's duty established in a contract to a third party	The party who makes an assignment of their rights

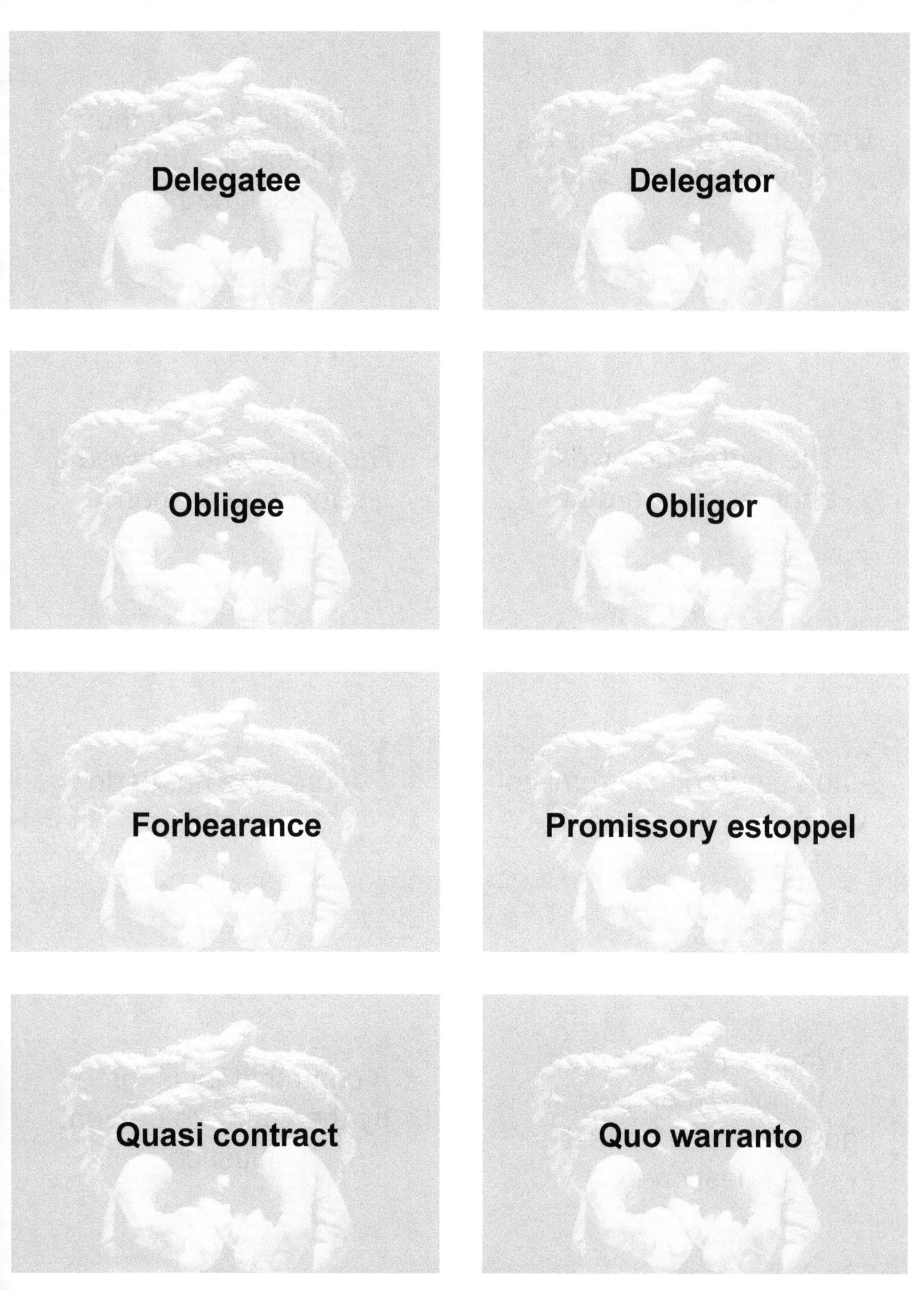

The party who assigns his duty to a third party	The third party the delegator's duty is assigned to
The party who owes another party a duty	The party who is owed a duty of performance
A non contractual promise which is still enforceable	A promise *not* to do something
When a persons right to hold an office or governmental benefit is questioned	A contract that is forced by the courts to prevent injustice

Uniform Commercial Code	1st Amendment
2nd Amendment	3rd Amendment
4th Amendment	5th Amendment
6th Amendment	Common Law

Freedom of religion, assembly, speech, press and freedom to petition	The law which governs contracts for sale of personal property
No quartering of soldiers	The right to keep and bear arms
The right to due process of law, freedom from self-incrimination, freedom from double jeopardy	Freedom from unreasonable searches and seizures
When the facts of a case are determined by judges and evaluated against previous cases that have similar facts to come to a decision by comparison	The right to a speedy and public trial

Six elements of a contract	Preexisting Duty
Imperfect obligations	Express acceptance
Termination of an offer	Unilateral mistake
Bilateral contract	Statute of Frauds

A promise to do what one person already has a legal duty to do	Offer, acceptance, capacity, consideration, mutual agreement, legality
When a person openly agrees to the offer, without doubts as to the acceptance	Are not binding on us as between two people, and for those non-performance of which we are accountable to God only; such as charity or gratitude
When only one party is mistaken	When an offer to a contract is withdrawn before acceptance, there is no contract
Contracts be documented in writing and that they be signed by all of the parties involved to make the contract to be enforceable and binding	Two promises, one by each party to the contract

MYLEGS	Repudiatory breach
Punitive damages	Compensatory damages
Rescission	Reformation
Waiver	Accord

A breach that is so fundamental that it allows the offended party the right to discontinue actions of the contract, along with the right to sue for damages	Marriage, year, land, executor, goods, suretyship
Aim to put the non-beaching party in the position that they had been if the breach had not occurred	Payments that the breaching party has to pay to compensate the non-breaching party
The terms of the contract are altered to clearly present the original intentions of both parties	The contract is mutually canceled and both sides are exempt from performance and money advanced is refunded
The agreement to accept a performance supplementary to that which was agreed upon under a previous contract	When one person voluntarily agrees to a request by another to give up his right of claim

www.ingramcontent.com/pod-product-compliance
Lightning Source LLC
Chambersburg PA
CBHW081830300426
44116CB00014B/2535